THE RETURN OF THE POLITICAL

THE RETURN OF THE POLITICAL

Chantal Mouffe

VERSO
London • New York

First published by Verso 1993
This edition published by Verso 2005
© Verso 1993, 2005

1 3 5 7 9 10 8 6 4 2

Verso
UK: 6 Meard Street, London W1F 0EG
USA: 180 Varick Street, New York NY 10014-4606
www.versobooks.com

Verso is the imprint of New Left Books

ISBN 1-84467-057-0

British Library Cataloguing in Publication Data
A catalogue record for this book is available from the British Library

Library of Congress Cataloging-in-Publication Data
A catalog record for this book is available from the Library of Congress

Printed and Bound in the United Kingdom by Bookmarque

Contents

Acknowledgements

The articles collected in this volume were originally published as follows: 'Radical Democracy: Modern or Postmodern?' in Andrew Ross, ed., *Universal Abandon? The Politics of Postmodernism*, University of Minnesota Press 1988; 'American Liberalism and its Communitarian Critics' (originally entitled 'American Liberalism and its Critics: Rawls, Taylor, Sandel and Walzer') in *Praxis International*, vol. 8, no. 2, July 1988; 'Rawls: Political Philosophy without Politics' in David Rasmussen, ed., *Universalism vs Communitarianism*, MIT Press 1990; 'Democratic Citizenship and the Political Community' in Chantal Mouffe, ed., *Dimensions of Radical Democracy*, Verso 1992; 'Feminism, Citizenship and Radical Democratic Politics' in Judith Butler and Joan Scott, *Feminists Theorize the Political*, Routledge 1992; 'Towards a Liberal Socialism' is the edited text of a paper presented at the World Congress of the International Political Science Association in Buenos Aires, Argentina, in July 1991; 'On the Articulation between Liberalism and Democracy' is the edited text of a paper presented at the conference 'The Legacy of C. B. Macpherson' in Toronto, Canada, in October 1989; 'Pluralism and Modern Democracy: Around Carl Schmitt' in *New Formations*, no. 14, Summer 1991; 'Politics and the Limits of Liberalism' was written for this volume.

Foreword

This volume brings together nine pieces written in the last five years. Some of them are articles already published, mostly in collective volumes; others are texts of presentations at conferences. The last one, 'Politics and the Limits of Liberalism' has been written especially for this book.

From different angles, all the essays deal with the same topics: radical democracy, liberalism, citizenship, pluralism, liberal democracy, community – which are here approached from an 'anti-essentialist' perspective.

The central theme that provides the unity of the book is a reflection on the political and on the ineradicable character of power and antagonism. I have tried to draw the consequences of such a reflection for a critique of the current rationalist and individualist liberal discourse, as well as for a reformulation of the left's project in terms of 'radical and plural democracy'.

Since the pieces were conceived for diverse audiences, there is obviously a certain amount of repetition due to the necessity of making the same points in different contexts. Nevertheless I decided to leave them in their original form because I consider that which is reiterated to be of the greatest importance.

Several of the essays were researched and written when I was a Member of the Institute for Advanced Study in Princeton in 1988–89 and a Senior Fellow at the Society for the Humanities at Cornell University in 1989–90. I am very grateful to both institutions for their support.

Alas, poor race of mortals, unhappy ones,
from what conflicts and what groans were you born

Empedocles

Introduction:
For an Agonistic
Pluralism

The trick is not to fool oneself about certain things: small rocky islands in the sea of self-deception. Clutching them and not drowning is the utmost that a human being achieves.

ELIAS CANETTI

1

Not long ago we were being told, to the accompaniment of much fanfare, that liberal democracy had won and that history had ended. Alas, far from having produced a smooth transition to pluralist democracy, the collapse of Communism seems, in many places, to have opened the way to a resurgence of nationalism and the emergence of new antagonisms. Western democrats view with astonishment the explosion of manifold ethnic, religious and nationalist conflicts that they thought belonged to a bygone age. Instead of the heralded 'New World Order', the victory of universal values, and the generalization of 'post-conventional' identities, we are witnessing an explosion of particularisms and an increasing challenge to Western universalism.

Taken by surprise by such a convincing refutation of their optimistic forecasts, many liberals have reacted by evoking the deferred effects of totalitarianism or a new upsurge of 'the archaic'. They respond as if it represented only a temporary delay on the road that necessarily leads to the universalization of liberal democracy: a short parenthesis before rationality reimposes its order, or a last desperate cry of the political before it is definitively destroyed by the forces of law and universal reason.

Because it is indeed the political which is at stake here, and the possibility of its elimination. And it is the incapacity of liberal thought to grasp its nature and the irreducible character of antagonism that

1

explains the impotence of most political theorists in the current situation – an impotence that, at a time of profound political change, could have devastating consequences for democratic politics.

2

This evasion of the political could, I believe, jeopardize the hard-won conquests of the democratic revolution, which is why, in the essays included in this volume, I take issue with the conception of politics that informs a great deal of democratic thinking today. This conception can be characterized as rationalist, universalist and individualist. I argue that its main shortcoming is that it cannot but remain blind to the specificity of the political in its dimension of conflict/decision, and that it cannot perceive the constitutive role of antagonism in social life. With the demise of Marxism, the illusion that we can finally dispense with the notion of antagonism has become widespread. This belief is fraught with danger, since it leaves us unprepared in the face of unrecognized manifestations of antagonism.

In an attempt to bring a much needed corrective to that liberal vision, several pieces below engage with the work of Carl Schmitt. Schmitt's critique of liberal democracy constitutes, in my view, a challenge that we cannot ignore. Yet I also think that, by revealing the deficiencies of liberalism, he can help us – unwittingly – to identify the issues that need to be addressed and thereby to gain a better understanding of the nature of modern democracy. My objective is to think with Schmitt, against Schmitt, and to use his insights in order to strengthen liberal democracy against his critiques. By drawing our attention to the centrality of the friend/enemy relation in politics, Schmitt makes us aware of the dimension of the political that is linked to the existence of an element of hostility among human beings. This can take many forms and manifest itself in very different types of social relations. This is an important idea, which I have tried to reformulate within the framework of the contemporary critique of essentialism that I take to constitute the most fruitful theoretical approach to pluralist democracy.

When we accept that every identity is relational and that the condition of existence of every identity is the affirmation of a difference, the determination of an 'other' that is going to play the role of a 'constitutive outside', it is possible to understand how antagonisms arise. In the domain of collective identifications, where what is in question is the creation of a 'we' by the delimitation of a 'them', the possibility always exists that this we/them relation will turn into a relation of the friend/enemy type; in other words, it can always become political in Schmitt's understanding of the term. This can happen when the other, who was until then considered only under the mode of difference, begins to be perceived as negating our identity, as putting in question our very existence. From that moment onwards, any type of we/them relation, be it religious, ethnic, national, economic or other, becomes the site of a political antagonism.

As a consequence, the political cannot be restricted to a certain type of institution, or envisaged as constituting a specific sphere or level of society. It must be conceived as a dimension that is inherent to every human society and that determines our very ontological condition. Such a view of the political is profoundly at odds with liberal thought, which is precisely the reason for the bewilderment of this thought when confronted with the phenomenon of hostility in its multiple forms. This is particularly evident in its incomprehension of political movements, which are seen as the expression of the so-called 'masses'. Since they cannot be apprehended in individualistic terms, these movements are usually relegated to the pathological or deemed to be the expression of irrational forces. Witness, for instance, the incapacity of liberal theorists to come to terms with the phenomenon of fascism.

3

On the eve of the twenty-first century, our societies are undergoing a deep process of redefinition of their collective identities and experiencing the establishment of new political frontiers. This is linked to the collapse of Communism and the disappearance of the democracy/totalitarianism opposition that, since the Second World War, had provided the main political frontier enabling discrimination between friend and enemy. This disappearance confronts us with a double situation:

1 In the former Communist bloc, the unity created in the common struggle against Communism has vanished and the friend/enemy frontier is taking a multiplicity of new forms linked to the resurgence of old antagonisms – ethnic, national, religious and others.

2 In the West, it is the very identity of democracy which is at stake, in so far as it has depended to a large extent on the existence of the Communist 'other' that constituted its negation. Now that the enemy has been defeated, the meaning of democracy itself has become

blurred and needs to be redefined by the creation of a new frontier. This is much more difficult for the moderate right and for the left than for the radical right. For the latter has already found its enemy. It is provided by the 'enemy within', the immigrants, which are presented by the different movements of the extreme right as a threat to the cultural identity and national sovereignty of the 'true' Europeans. I submit that the growth of the extreme right in several countries in Europe can only be understood in the context of the deep crisis of political identity that confronts liberal democracy following the loss of the traditional landmarks of politics. It is linked to the necessity of redrawing the political frontier between friend and enemy.

4

We are in a conjuncture where the incapacity of liberalism to apprehend the political could have very serious consequences. All those who believed that the fall of Communism would necessarily be followed by the establishment of pluralist democracy, and that the destruction of the old antagonist could only herald a great advance for democracy, are quite unable to understand the specificity of the new situation. For that reason, it is vital that we abandon a theoretical perspective that prevents us coming to terms with the nature of the tasks before us.

Once we accept the necessity of the political and the impossibility of a world without antagonism, what needs to be envisaged is how it is possible *under those conditions* to create or maintain a pluralistic democratic order. Such an order is based on a distinction between 'enemy' and 'adversary'. It requires that, within the context of the political community, the opponent should be considered not as an enemy to be destroyed, but as an adversary whose existence is legitimate and must be tolerated. We will fight against his ideas but we will not question his right to defend them. The category of the 'enemy' does not disappear but is displaced; it remains pertinent with respect to those who do not accept the democratic 'rules of the game' and who thereby exclude themselves from the political community.

Liberal democracy requires consensus on the rules of the game, but it also calls for the constitution of collective identities around clearly differentiated positions and the possibility of choosing between real alternatives. This 'agonistic pluralism' is constitutive of modern democracy and, rather than seeing it as a threat, we should realize that it represents the very condition of existence of such democracy.

Niklas Luhmann has argued that the specificity of liberal democracy as a political system is the 'splitting of the summit' – the distinction between government and opposition. He specifies that 'This presupposes a corresponding binary oppositional programming – e.g. conservative/progressive or, since that does not work any more, restrictive/expansive welfare state policies or, if the economy does not permit this, then ecological versus economic preferences. Only in this way can possible directions of the political course be put to choice.'[1] This means that the current blurring of political frontiers between left and right is harmful for democratic politics, as it impedes the constitution of distinctive political identities. This in turn fosters disaffection towards political parties and discourages participation in the political process. Hence the growth of other collective identities around religious, nationalist or ethnic forms of identification.

This confirms, as Schmitt has pointed out, that antagonisms can take many forms, and it is illusory to believe they could ever be eliminated. In those circumstances, it is preferable to give them a political outlet within a pluralistic democratic system. The great strength of liberal democracy, *pace* Schmitt, is precisely that it provides the institutions that, if properly understood, can shape the element of hostility in a way that defuses its potential. Indeed, as Elias Canetti shows in *Crowds and Power*, the parliamentary system exploits the psychological structure of struggling armies and should be conceived as a struggle in which the contending parties renounce the killing of each other and accept the verdict of the majority on who has won. According to him, '[T]he actual vote is decisive, as the moment in which the one is really measured against the other. It is all that is left of the original lethal clash and it is played out in many forms, with threats, abuse and physical provocation which may lead to blows or missiles. But the counting of the vote ends the battle.'[2] If we accept such a view, it follows that parties can play an important role in giving expression to social division and the conflict of wills. But if they fail in their job, conflicts will assume other guises and it will be more difficult to manage them democratically.

5

The illusion of consensus and unanimity, as well as the calls for 'antipolitics', should be recognized as being fatal for democracy and therefore abandoned. The absence of a political frontier, far from being a sign of political maturity, is the symptom of a void that can endanger democracy, because that void provides a terrain that can be occupied by the extreme right to articulate new antidemocratic political identities. When there is a lack of democratic political struggles with which to identify, their place is taken by other forms of identification, of ethnic, nationalist or religious nature, and the opponent is defined in those terms too. In such conditions, the opponent cannot be perceived as an adversary to contend with, but only as an enemy to be destroyed. This is precisely what a pluralist democracy must avoid; yet it can only protect itself against such a situation by recognizing the nature of the political instead of denying its existence.

To acknowledge that 'the state of nature' in its Hobbesian dimension can never be completely eradicated but only controlled, throws a different light on the status of democracy. Far from being the necessary result of a moral evolution of humankind, democracy is something uncertain and improbable and must never be taken for granted. It is an always fragile conquest that needs to be defended as well as deepened. There is no threshold of democracy that once reached will guarantee its continued existence. Democracy is in peril not only when there is insufficient consensus and allegiance to the values it embodies, but also when its agonistic dynamic is hindered by an apparent excess of consensus, which usually masks a disquieting apathy. It is also endangered by the growing marginalization of entire groups whose status as an 'underclass' practically puts them outside the political community.

When, as is the case today, liberal democracy is increasingly identified with 'actually existing liberal democratic capitalism', and its political dimension is restricted to the rule of law, there is a risk that the excluded may join fundamentalist movements or become attracted to antiliberal, populist forms of democracy. A healthy democratic process calls for a vibrant clash of political positions and an open conflict of interests. If such is missing, it can too easily be replaced by a confrontation between non-negotiable moral values and essentialist identities.

6

Nowadays, the crucial issue is how to establish a new political frontier capable of giving a real impulse to democracy. I believe that this requires redefining the left as a horizon where the many different struggles against subordination could find a space of inscription. The notion of a radical democratic citizenship is crucial here because it could provide a form of identification that enables the establishment of a common political identity among diverse democratic struggles. There are currently many attempts on the left to recover the idea of citizenship but, as I argue in several pieces below, it is important not to aim at a neutral conception of citizenship applicable to all members of the political community. This is why, while being attentive to its critique of liberal individualism, I am wary of many aspects of the communitarian approach. Its rejection of pluralism and defence of a substantive idea of the 'common good' represents, in my view, another way of evading the ineluctability of antagonism. There will always be competing interpretations of the political principles of liberal democracy, and the meanings of liberty and equality will never cease to be contested. Citizenship is vital for democratic politics, but a modern democratic theory must make room for competing conceptions of our identities as citizens.

From different angles, the essays collected here all seek to develop various aspects of the project of 'radical and plural democracy' put forward in *Hegemony and Socialist Strategy*.[3] In stressing the centrality of the idea of pluralism for modern democracy, I recognize the latter's debt to the liberal tradition. One of my main theses, though, is that in order to develop fully the potentialities of the liberal ideals of individual freedom and personal autonomy, we need to dissociate them from the other discourses to which they have been articulated and to rescue political liberalism from its association with economic liberalism.

I argue that, in order to radicalize the idea of pluralism, so as to make it a vehicle for a deepening of the democratic revolution, we have to break with rationalism, individualism and universalism. Only on that condition will it be possible to apprehend the multiplicity of forms of subordination that exist in social relations and to provide a framework for the articulation of the different democratic struggles – around gender, race, class, sexuality, environment and others. This does not imply the rejection of any idea of rationality, individuality or universality, but affirms that they are necessarily plural, discursively constructed and entangled with power relations. It means acknowledging the existence of the political in its complexity: the dimension of the 'we', the construction of the friend's side, as well as the dimension of the 'them', the constitutive aspect of antagonism. This is why such pluralism must also be distinguished from the postmodern conception of the fragmentation of the social, which refuses to grant the fragments any kind of relational identity. The perspective I maintain consistently rejects any kind of essentialism – either of the totality or of the elements – and affirms that neither the totality nor the fragments possess any kind of fixed identity, prior to the contingent and pragmatic form of their articulation.

It is because it does not try to negate the political that, contrary to other conceptions of radical or participatory democracy informed by a universalistic and rationalist framework, the view I am advocating here is truly one of radical and *plural* democracy. It is the only conception that draws the full implications of the 'pluralism of values' and confronts the consequences of acknowledging the permanence of conflict and antagonism. From such a standpoint, conflicts are not seen as disturbances that unfortunately cannot be eliminated, as empirical impediments that render impossible the full realization of harmony due to the fact that we will never completely coincide with our rational · universal self. For a radical and plural democracy, the belief that a final resolution of conflicts is eventually possible, even if envisaged as an asymptotic approach to the regulative ideal of a free and unconstrained communication, as in Habermas, far from providing the necessary horizon of the democratic project, is something that puts it at risk.

Central to this approach is the awareness that a pluralist democracy contains a paradox, since the very moment of its realization would see its disintegration. It should be conceived as a good that only exists as good so long as it cannot be reached. Such a democracy will therefore always be a democracy 'to come', as conflict and antagonism are at the same time its condition of possibility and the condition of impossibility of its full realization.

Notes

1. Niklas Luhmann, 'The Future of Democracy', *Thesis Eleven*, no. 26, 1990, p. 51.
2. Elias Canetti, *Crowds and Power*, London 1973, p. 220.
3. Ernesto Laclau and Chantal Mouffe, *Hegemony and Socialist Strategy. Towards a Radical Democratic Politics*, London 1985.

1

Radical Democracy:
Modern or Postmodern?

What does it mean to be on the left today? In the twilight years of the twentieth century is it in any way meaningful to invoke the Enlightenment ideals that lay behind the project of the transformation of society? We are undoubtedly living through the crisis of the Jacobin imaginary, which has, in diverse ways, characterized the revolutionary politics of the last two hundred years. It is unlikely that Marxism will recover from the blows it has suffered; not only the discredit brought upon the Soviet model by the analysis of totalitarianism, but also the challenge to class reductionism posed by the emergence of new social movements. But the fraternal enemy, the social democratic movement, is not in any better shape. It has proved incapable of addressing the new demands of recent decades, and its central achievement, the welfare state, has held up badly under attack from the right, because it has not been able to mobilize those who should have interests in defending its achievements.

As for the ideal of socialism, what seems to be in question is the very idea of progress that is bound up with the project of modernity. In this respect, discussion of the postmodern, which until now had focused on culture, has taken a political turn. Alas, the debate all too quickly petrified around a set of simplistic and sterile positions. Whereas Habermas accuses of conservatism all those who criticize the universalist ideal of the Enlightenment,[1] Lyotard declares with pathos that after Auschwitz the project of modernity has been eliminated.[2] Richard Rorty rightly remarks that one finds on both sides an illegitimate assimilation of the political project of the Enlightenment and its epistemological aspects. This is why Lyotard finds it necessary to abandon political liberalism in order to avoid a universalist philosophy, whereas Habermas, who wants to defend liberalism, holds on, despite all of its problems, to this universalist philosophy.[3] Habermas indeed believes that the emergence of universalist forms of

9

morality and law is the expression of an irreversible collective process of learning, and that to reject this implies a rejection of modernity, undermining the very foundations of democracy's existence. Rorty invites us to consider Blumenberg's distinction, in *The Legitimacy of the Modern Age*, between two aspects of the Enlightenment, t..at of 'self-assertion' (which can be identified with the political project) and that of 'self-foundation' (the epistemological project). Once we acknowledge that there is no necessary relation between these two aspects, we are in the position of being able to defend the political project while abandoning the notion that it must be based on a specific form of rationality.

Rorty's position, however, is problematic because of his identification of the political project of modernity with a vague concept of 'liberalism' which includes both capitalism and democracy. For, at the heart of the very concept of political modernity, it is important to distinguish two traditions, liberal and democratic, both of which, as Macpherson has shown, are articulated only in the nineteenth century and are thus not necessarily related in any way. Moreover, it would be a mistake to confuse this 'political modernity' with 'social modernity', the process of modernization carried out under the growing domination of relations of capitalist production. If one fails to draw this distinction between democracy and liberalism, between political liberalism and economic liberalism; if, as Rorty does, one conflates all these notions under the term *liberalism*; then one is driven, under the pretext of defending modernity, to a pure and simple apology for the 'institutions and practices of the rich North Atlantic democracies',[4] which leaves no room for a critique (not even an immanent critique) that would enable us to transform them.

Confronted by this 'postmodernist bourgeois liberalism' that Rorty advocates, I would like to show how the project of a 'radical and plural democracy', one that Ernesto Laclau and I have already sketched out in our book *Hegemony and Socialist Strategy: Towards a Radical Democratic Politics*,[5] proposes a reformulation of the socialist project that avoids the twin pitfalls of Marxist socialism and social democracy, while providing the left with a new imaginary, an imaginary that speaks to the tradition of the great emancipatory struggles but that also takes into account recent theoretical contributions by psychoanalysis and philosophy. In effect, such a project could be defined as being both modern and postmodern. It pursues the 'unfulfilled project of modernity', but, unlike Habermas, we believe that there is no longer a role to be played in this project by the epistemological perspective of the Enlightenment. Although this perspective did play an important part in the emergence of democracy, it has become an obstacle in the path of understanding those new forms of politics, characteristic of our societies today, which demand to be approached from a nonessentialist perspective. Hence the necessity of using the theoretical tools elaborated by the different currents of what can be called the postmodern in philosophy and of appropriating their critique of rationalism and subjectivism.[6]

The Democratic Revolution

A number of different criteria have been suggested for defining modernity. They vary a great deal depending on the particular levels or features one wants to emphasize. I, for one, think that modernity must be defined at the political level, for it is there that social relations take shape and are symbolically ordered. In so far as it inaugurates a new type of society, modernity can be viewed as a decisive point of reference. In this respect the fundamental characteristic of modernity is undoubtedly the advent of the democratic revolution. As Claude Lefort has shown, this democratic revolution is at the origin of a new kind of institution of the social, in which power becomes an 'empty place'. For this reason, modern democratic society is constituted as 'a society in which power, law and knowledge are exposed to a radical indetermination, a society that has become the theatre of an uncontrollable adventure, so that what is instituted never becomes established, the known remains undetermined by the unknown, the present proves to be undefinable.'[7] The absence of power embodied in the person of the prince and tied to a transcendental authority pre-empts the existence of a final guarantee or source of legitimation; society can no longer be defined as a substance having an organic identity. What remains is a society without clearly defined outlines, a social structure that is impossible to describe from the perspective of a single, or universal, point of view. It is in this way that democracy is characterized by the 'dissolution of the markers of certainty'.[8] I think that such an approach is extremely suggestive and useful because it allows us to put many of the phenomena of modern societies in a new perspective. Thus, the effects of the democratic revolution can be analysed in the arts, theory, and all aspects of culture in general, enabling one to formulate the question of the relation between modernity and postmodernity in a new and more productive way. Indeed, if one sees the democratic revolution as Lefort portrays it, as the distinctive feature of modernity, it then becomes clear that what one means when one refers to postmodernity in philosophy is a recognition of the impossibility of any ultimate foundation or final legitimation that is constitutive of the very advent of the democratic form of society and thus of modernity itself. This recognition comes after the failure of several attempts to replace the traditional foundation that lay within God or Nature with an alternative foundation lying in Man and his Reason. These attempts were doomed to failure from the start because of the radical indeterminacy that is characteristic of modern democracy. Nietzsche had already understood this when he proclaimed that the death of God was inseparable from the crisis of humanism.[9]

Therefore the challenge to rationalism and humanism does not imply the rejection of modernity but only the crisis of a particular project within modernity, the Enlightenment project of self-foundation. Nor does it imply that we have to abandon its political project, which is the achievement of equality and freedom for all. In order to pursue and deepen this aspect of the democratic revolution, we must ensure that the democratic project takes account of the full breadth and specificity of the democratic struggles in our times. It is here that the contribution of the so-called postmodern critique comes into its own.

How, in effect, can we hope to understand the nature of these new antagonisms if we hold on to an image of the unitary subject as the ultimate source of intelligibility of its actions? How can we grasp the multiplicity of relations of subordination that can affect an individual if we envisage social agents as homogeneous and unified entities? What characterizes the struggles of these new social movements is precisely the multiplicity of subject positions which constitute a single agent and the possibility that this multiplicity can become the site of an antagonism and thereby politicized. Hence the importance of the critique of the rationalist concept of a unitary subject, which one finds not only in post-structuralism but also in psychoanalysis, in the philosophy of language of the late Wittgenstein, and in Gadamer's hermeneutics.

To be capable of thinking politics today, and understanding the nature of these new struggles and the diversity of social relations that the democratic revolution has yet to encompass, it is indispensable to develop a theory of the subject as a decentred, detotalized agent, a subject constructed at the point of intersection of a multiplicity of subject positions between which there exists no a priori or necessary relation and whose articulation is the result of hegemonic practices. Consequently, no identity is ever definitively established, there always being a certain degree of openness and ambiguity in the way the different subject positions are articulated. What emerges are entirely new perspectives for political action, which neither liberalism, with its idea of the individual who only pursues his or her own interest, nor Marxism, with its reduction of all subject positions to that of class, can sanction, let alone imagine.

It should be noted, then, that this new phase of the democratic revolution, while being, in its own way, a result of the democratic universalism of the Enlightenment, also puts into question some of its assumptions. Many of these new struggles do in fact renounce any claim to universality. They show how in every assertion of universality there lies a disavowal of the particular and a refusal of specificity. Feminist criticism unmasks the particularism hiding behind those so-called universal ideals which, in fact, have always been mechanisms of exclusion. Carole Pateman, for example, has shown how classical theories of democracy were based upon the exclusion of women: 'The idea of universal citizenship is specifically modern, and necessarily depends on the emergence of the view that all individuals are born free and equal, or are naturally free and equal to each other. No individual is naturally subordinate to another, and all must thus have public standing as citizens, that upholds their self-governing status. Individual freedom and equality also entails that government can arise only through agreement or consent. We are all taught that the "individual" is a universal category that applies to anyone or everyone, but this is not the case. "The individual" is a man.'[10]

The reformulation of the democratic project in terms of radical democracy requires giving up the abstract Enlightenment universalism of an undifferentiated human nature. Even though the emergence of the first theories of modern democracy and of the individual as a bearer of rights was made possible by these very concepts, they have today become a major obstacle to the future extension of the democratic revolution. The new rights that are being claimed today are the expression of differences whose importance is only now being asserted, and they are no longer rights that can be universalized. Radical democracy demands that we acknowledge difference – the particular, the multiple, the heterogeneous – in effect, everything that had been excluded by the concept of Man in the abstract. Universalism is not rejected but particularized; what is needed is a new kind of articulation between the universal and the particular.

Practical Reason: Aristotle versus Kant

This increasing dissatisfaction with the abstract universalism of the Enlightenment explains the rehabilitation of the Aristotelian concept of *phronesis*. This 'ethical knowledge', distinct from the knowledge specific to the sciences (*episteme*), is dependent on the ethos, the cultural and historical conditions current in the community, and implies a renunciation of all pretence to universality.[11] This is a kind of rationality proper to the study of human praxis, which excludes all possibility of a 'science' of practice but which demands the existence of a 'practical reason', a region not characterized by apodictic statements, where the reasonable prevails over the demonstrable. Kant brought forth a very different notion of practical reason, one that required universality. As Ricoeur observes: 'By elevating to the rank of supreme principle the rule of universalisation, Kant inaugurated one of the most dangerous ideas which was to prevail from Fichte to Marx; that the practical sphere was to be subject to a scientific kind of knowledge comparable to the scientific knowledge required in the theoretical sphere.'[12] So, too, Gadamer criticizes Kant for having opened the way to positivism in the human sciences and considers the Aristotelian notion of *phronesis* to be much more adequate than the Kantian analysis of judgement to grasp the kind of relation existing between the universal and the particular in the sphere of human action.[13]

The development of the postempiricist philosophy of science converges with hermeneutics to challenge the positivistic model of rationality dominant in the sciences. Theorists such as Thomas Kuhn and Mary Hesse have contributed a great deal to this critique by pointing to the importance of rhetorical elements in the evolution of science. It is agreed today that we need to broaden the concept of rationality to make room for the 'reasonable' and the 'plausible' and to recognize the existence of multiple forms of rationality.

Such ideas are crucial to the concept of a radical democracy in which judgement plays a fundamental role that must be conceptualized appropriately so as to avoid the false dilemmas between, on the one hand, the existence of some universal criterion and, on the other, the rule of arbitrariness. That a question remains unanswerable by science or that it does not attain the status of a truth that can be demonstrated does not mean that a reasonable opinion cannot be formed about it or that it cannot be an opportunity for a rational choice. Hannah Arendt was absolutely right to insist that in the political sphere one finds oneself in the realm of opinion , or 'doxa', and not in that of truth, and that each sphere has its own criteria of validity and legitimacy.[14] There are those, of course, who will argue that such a position is haunted by the spectre of relativism. But such an accusation makes sense only if one remains in the thrall of a traditional problematic which offers no alternative between objectivism and relativism.

To assert that one cannot provide an ultimate rational foundation for any given system of values does not imply that one considers all views to be equal. As Rorty notes, 'the real issue is not between people who think one view as good as any other and people who do not. It is between people who think our culture, our purpose or institutions cannot be supported except conversationally and people who still hope for other sorts of support.'[15] It is always possible to distinguish between the just and the unjust, the legitimate and the illegitimate, but this can only be done from within a given tradition, with the help of standards that this tradition provides; in fact, there is no point of view external to all tradition from which one can offer a universal judgement. Furthermore, to give up the distinction between logic and rhetoric to which the postmodern critique leads – and where it parts with Aristotle – does not mean that 'might makes right' or that one sinks into nihilism. To accept with Foucault that there cannot be an absolute separation between validity and power (since validity is always relative to a specific regime of truth, connected to power) does not mean that we cannot distinguish within a given regime of truth between those who respect the strategy of argumentation and its rules, and those who simply want to impose their power.

Finally, the absence of foundation 'leaves everything as it is', as Wittgenstein would say, and obliges us to ask the same questions in a new way. Hence the error of a certain kind of apocalyptical postmodernism which would like us to believe that we are at the threshold of a radically new epoch, characterized by drift, dissemination, and the uncontrollable play of significations. Such a view remains the captive of a rationalistic problematic, which it attempts to criticize. As has been pointed out: 'The real mistake of the classical meta-physician was not the belief that there were metaphysical foundations, but rather the belief that somehow or other such foundations were necessary, the belief that unless there are foundations something is lost or threatened or undermined or just in question.'[16]

Tradition and Democratic Politics

Because of the importance it accords to the particular, to the existence of different forms of rationality, and to the role of tradition, the path of radical democracy paradoxically runs across some of the main currents of conservative thinking. One of the chief emphases of conservative thought does indeed lie in its critique of the Enlightenment's rationalism and universalism, a critique it shares with postmodernist thought; this proximity might explain why certain postmodernists have been branded as conservative by Habermas. In fact, the affinities can be found not on the level of the political but in the fact that, unlike liberalism and Marxism, both of which are doctrines of reconciliation and mastery, conservative philosophy is predicated upon human finitude, imperfection and limits. This does not lead unavoidably to a defence of the status quo and to an antidemocratic vision, for it lends itself to various kinds of articulation.

The notion of tradition, for example, has to be distinguished from that of traditionalism. Tradition allows us to think our own insertion into historicity, the fact that we are constructed as subjects through a series of already existing discourses, and that it is through this tradition which forms us that the world is given to us and all political action made possible. A conception of politics like that of Michael Oakeshott, who attributes a central role to the existing 'traditions of behavior' and who sees political action as 'the pursuit of an intimation', is very useful and productive for the formulation of radical democracy. Indeed, for Oakeshott, 'Politics is the activity of attending to the general arrangements of a collection of people who, in respect of their common recognition of a manner of attending to its arrangements, compose a single community. . . . This activity, then, springs neither from instant desires, nor from general principles, but from the existing traditions of behavior themselves. And the form it takes, because it can take no other, is the amendment of existing arrangements by exploring and pursuing what is intimated in them.'[17] If one considers the liberal democratic tradition to be the main tradition of behaviour in our societies, one can understand the extension of the democratic revolution and development of struggles for equality and liberty in every area of social life as being the pursuit of these 'intimations' present in liberal democratic discourse. Oakeshott provides us with a good example, while unaware of the radical potential of his arguments. Discussing the legal status of women, he declares that 'the arrangements which constitute a society capable of political activity, whether these are customs or institutions or laws or diplomatic decisions, are at once coherent and incoherent; they compose a pattern and at the same time they intimate a sympathy for what does not fully appear. Political activity is the exploration of that sympathy; and consequently, relevant political reasoning will be convincing exposure of a sympathy, present but not yet followed up, and the convincing demonstration that now is the appropriate moment for recognizing it.'[18] He concludes that it is in this way that one is capable of recognizing the legal equality of women. It is immediately apparent how useful reasoning of this kind can be as a justification of the extension of democratic principles.

This importance afforded to tradition is also one of the principal themes of Gadamer's philosophical hermeneutics, which offers us a number of important ways of thinking about the construction of the political subject. Following Heidegger, Gadamer asserts the existence of a fundamental unity between thought, language and the world. It is through language that the horizon of our present is constituted; this language bears the mark of the past; it is the life of the past in the present and thus constitutes the movement of tradition. The error of the Enlightenment, according to Gadamer, was to discredit 'prejudices' and to propose an ideal of understanding which requires that one transcend one's present and free oneself from one's insertion into history. But it is precisely these prejudices that define our hermeneutical situation and constitute our condition of understanding and openness to the world. Gadamer also rejects the opposition drawn up by the Enlightenment between tradition and reason, because for him 'tradition is constantly an element of freedom and of history itself. Even the most genuine and solid tradition does not persist by nature because of the inertia of what once existed. It needs to be affirmed, embraced, cultivated. It is, essentially, preservation such as is active in all historical change. But preservation is an act of reason, though an unconspicuous one. For this reason, only what is new, or what is planned, appears as the result of reason. But this is an illusion. Even where life changes violently, as in ages of revolution, far more of the old is preserved in the supposed transformation of everything than anyone knows, and combines with the new to create a new value.'[19]

This conception of tradition found in Gadamer can be made more specific and complex if reformulated in terms of Wittgenstein's 'language games'. Seen in this light, tradition becomes the set of language games that make up a given community. Since for Wittgenstein language games are an indissoluble union between linguistic rules, objective situations and forms of life,[20] tradition is the set of discourses and practices that form us as subjects. Thus we are able to think of politics as the pursuit of intimations, which in a Wittgensteinian perspective can be understood as the creation of new usages for the key terms of a given tradition, and of their use in new language games that make new forms of life possible.

To be able to think about the politics of radical democracy through the notion of tradition, it is important to emphasize the composite, heterogeneous, open, and ultimately indeterminate character of the democratic tradition. Several possible strategies are always available, not only in the sense of the different interpretations one can make of the same element, but also because of the way in which some parts or aspects of tradition can be played against others. This is what Gramsci, perhaps the only Marxist to have understood the role of tradition, saw as a process of disarticulation and rearticulation of elements characteristic of hegemonic practices.[21]

Recent attempts by neoliberals and neoconservatives to redefine concepts such as liberty and equality, and to disarticulate the idea of liberty from that of democracy, demonstrate how within the liberal democratic tradition different strategies can be pursued, making available different kinds of intimations. Confronted by this offensive on the part of those who want to put an end to the articulation that was established in the nineteenth century between liberalism and democracy and who want to redefine liberty as nothing more than an absence of coercion, the project of radical democracy must try to defend democracy and to expand its sphere of applicability to new social relations. It aims to create another kind of articulation between elements of the liberal democratic tradition, no longer viewing rights in an individualist framework but rather conceiving of 'democratic rights'. This will create a new hegemony, which will be the outcome of the articulation of the greatest possible number of democratic struggles.

What we need is a hegemony of democratic values, and this requires a multiplication of democratic practices, institutionalizing them into ever more diverse social relations, so that a multiplicity of subject positions can be formed through a democratic matrix. It is in this way – and not by trying to provide it with a rational foundation – that we will be able not only to defend democracy but also to deepen it. Such a hegemony will never be complete, and anyway, it is not desirable for a society to be ruled by a single democratic logic. Relations of authority and power cannot completely disappear, and it is important to abandon the myth of a transparent society, reconciled with itself, for that kind of fantasy leads to totalitarianism. A project of radical and plural democracy, on the contrary, requires the existence of multiplicity, of plurality and of conflict, and sees in them the *raison d'être* of politics.

Radical Democracy, a New Political Philosophy

If the task of radical democracy is indeed to deepen the democratic revolution and to link diverse democratic struggles, such a task requires the creation of new subject positions that would allow the common articulation, for example, of antiracism, antisexism and anticapitalism. These struggles do not spontaneously converge, and in order to establish democratic equivalences a new 'common sense' is necessary, which would transform the identity of different groups so that the demands of each group could be articulated with those of others according to the principle of democratic equivalence. For it is not a matter of establishing a mere alliance between given interests but of actually modifying the very identity of these forces. In order that the defence of workers' interests is not pursued at the cost of the rights of women, immigrants or consumers, it is necessary to establish an equivalence between these different struggles. It is only under these circumstances that struggles against power become truly democratic.

Political philosophy has a very important role to play in the emergence of this common sense and in the creation of these new subject positions, for it will shape the 'definition of reality' that will provide the form of political experience and serve as a matrix for the construction of a certain kind of subject. Some of the key concepts of liberalism, such as rights, liberty and citizenship, are claimed today by the discourse of possessive individualism, which stands in the way of the establishment of a chain of democratic equivalences.

I have already referred to the necessity of a concept of democratic rights: rights which, while belonging to the individual, can only be exercised collectively and which presuppose the existence of equal rights for others. But radical democracy also needs an idea of liberty that transcends the false dilemma between the liberty of the ancients and the moderns and allows us to think individual liberty and political liberty together. On this issue, radical democracy shares the pre-occupations of various writers who want to redeem the tradition of civic republicanism. This trend is quite heterogeneous, and it is therefore necessary to draw distinctions among the so-called communitarians who, while they all share a critique of liberal individualism's idea of a subject existing prior to the social relations that form it, have differing attitudes toward modernity. On the one hand, there are those like Michael Sandel and Alasdair MacIntyre, inspired mainly by Aristotle, who reject liberal pluralism in the name of a politics of the common good, and, on the other hand, those like Charles Taylor and Michael Walzer, who, while they criticize the epistemological presuppositions of liberalism, try to incorporate its political contribution in the area of rights and pluralism.[22] The latter hold a perspective closer to that of radical democracy, whereas the former maintain an extremely ambiguous attitude toward the advent of democracy and tend to defend premodern conceptions of politics, drawing no distinctions between the ethical and the political, which they understand as the expression of shared moral values.

It is probably in the work of Machiavelli that civic republicanism has

the most to offer us, and in this respect the recent work of Quentin
Skinner is of particular interest. Skinner shows that in Machiavelli one
finds a conception of liberty that, although it does not postulate an
objective notion of the good life (and therefore is, according to Isaiah
Berlin, a 'negative' conception of liberty), nevertheless includes ideals
of political participation and civic virtue (which, according to Berlin,
are typical of a 'positive' conception of liberty). Skinner shows that the
idea of liberty is portrayed in the *Discourses* as the capacity for
individuals to pursue their own goals, their 'humors' (*humori*). This
goes together with the affirmation that in order to ensure the necessary
conditions for avoiding coercion and servitude, thereby rendering
impossible the use of this liberty, it is indispensable for individuals to
fulfil certain public functions and to cultivate required virtues. For
Machiavelli, if one is to exercise civic virtue and serve the common
good, it is in order to guarantee oneself a certain degree of personal
liberty which permits one to pursue one's own ends.[23] We encounter
in this a very modern conception of individual liberty articulated onto
an old conception of political liberty, which is fundamental for the
development of a political philosophy of radical democracy.

But this appeal to a tradition of civic republicanism, even in the
privileging of its Machiavellian branch, cannot wholly provide us with
the political language needed for an articulation of the multiplicity of
today's democratic struggles. The best it can do is provide us with
elements to fight the negative aspects of liberal individualism, while it
remains inadequate to grasp the complexity of politics today. Our
societies are confronted with the proliferation of political spaces which
are radically new and different and which demand that we abandon
the idea of a unique constitutive space of the constitution of the
political, which is particular to both liberalism and civic republicanism.
If the liberal conception of the 'unencumbered self' is deficient, the
alternative presented by the communitarian defenders of civic
republicanism is unsatisfactory as well. It is not question of moving
from a 'unitary unencumbered self' to a 'unitary situated self'; the
problem is with the very idea of the unitary subject. Many
communitarians seem to believe that we belong to only one
community, defined empirically and even geographically, and that
this community could be unified by a single idea of the common good.
But we are in fact always multiple and contradictory subjects,
inhabitants of a diversity of communities (as many, really, as the social
relations in which we participate and the subject positions they
define), constructed by a variety of discourses, and precariously and
temporarily sutured at the intersection of those subject positions.
Hence the importance of the postmodern critique for developing a

political philosophy aimed at making possible a new form of individuality that would be truly plural and democratic. A philosophy of this sort does not assume a rational foundation for democracy, nor does it provide answers, in the way of Leo Strauss, to questions concerning the nature of political matters and the best regime. On the contrary, it proposes to remain with the cave and, as Michael Walzer puts it, 'to interpret to one's fellow citizens the world of meanings that we share.'[24] The liberal democratic tradition is open to many interpretations, and the politics of radical democracy is but one strategy among others. Nothing guarantees its success, but this project has set out to pursue and deepen the democratic project of modernity. Such a strategy requires us to abandon the abstract universalism of the Enlightenment, the essentialist conception of a social totality, and the myth of a unitary subject. In this respect, far from seeing the development of postmodern philosophy as a threat, radical democracy welcomes it as an indispensable instrument in the accomplishment of its goals.

Translated by Paul Holdengräber

Notes

1. Jürgen Habermas, 'Modernity – An Incomplete Project', in Hal Foster, ed., *The Anti-Aesthetic: Essays on Postmodern Culture*, Port Townsend 1983.

2. Jean-François Lyotard, *Immaterialitat und Postmoderne*, Berlin 1985.

3. Richard Rorty, 'Habermas and Lyotard on Postmodernity', in Richard J. Bernstein, ed., *Habermas and Modernity*, Oxford 1985, pp. 161–75.

4. Richard Rorty, 'Postmodernist Bourgeois Liberalism', *Journal of Philosophy*, 80, October 1983, p. 585.

5. Ernesto Laclau and Chantal Mouffe, *Hegemony and Socialist Strategy: Towards a Radical Democratic Politics*, London 1985.

6. I am referring not only to post-structuralism but also to other trends like psychoanalysis, post-Heideggerian hermeneutics and the philosophy of language of the second Wittgenstein, which all converge in a critique of rationalism and subjectivism.

7. Claude Lefort, *The Political Forms of Modern Society*, Oxford 1986, p. 305.

8. Claude Lefort, *Democracy and Political Theory*, Oxford 1988, p. 19.

9. On this issue, see the insightful analysis of Gianni Vattimo, 'La crisi dell "umanismo"', in *La fine della modernita*, Milan 1985, ch..2.

10. Carole Pateman, 'Removing Obstacles to Democracy', paper presented to the International Political Science Association meeting, Ottawa, Canada, October 1986, mimeographed.

11. Recent interpretations of Aristotle try to dissociate him from the tradition of natural law and to underline the differences between him and Plato on this issue. See, for instance, Hans-Georg Gadamer's remarks in *Truth and Method*, New York 1984, pp. 278–89.

12. Paul Ricoeur, *Du texte à l'action*, Paris 1986, pp. 248–51.

13. Gadamer, *Truth and Method*, pp. 33–39.

14. Hannah Arendt, *Between Past and Future*, New York 1968.

15. Richard Rorty, *Consequences of Pragmatism*, Minneapolis 1982, p. 167.

16. John R. Searle, 'The Word Turned Upside Down', *The New York Review of Books*, 27 October 1983, p. 78.

17. Michael Oakeshott, *Rationalism in Politics*, London 1967, p. 123.

18. Ibid., p. 124.

19. Gadamer, *Truth and Method*, p. 250.

20. Ludwig Wittgenstein, *Philosophical Investigations*, Oxford 1953.

21. On this issue, see my article 'Hegemony and Ideology in Gramsci', in Chantal Mouffe, ed., *Gramsci and Marxist Theory*, London 1979, pp. 168–204.

22. I refer here to the following studies: Michael Sandel, *Liberalism and the Limits of Justice*, Cambridge 1982; Alasdair MacIntyre, *After Virtue*, Notre Dame 1984; Charles Taylor, *Philosophy and the Human Sciences*, Philosophical Papers 2, Cambridge 1985; Michael Walzer, *Spheres of Justice*, New York 1983.

23. Quentin Skinner, 'The Idea of Negative Liberty: Philosophical and Historical Perspectives', in R. Rorty, J. B. Schneewind and Q. Skinner, eds, *Philosophy in History*, Cambridge 1984.

24. Walzer, *Spheres of Justice*, p. xiv.

American Liberalism
and its Communitarian
Critics

Since Tocqueville, the United States has often been considered the preferred land of liberal democracy, which, starting from the constitution of 1787, could have blossomed without encountering the obstacles that it had to overcome in the European countries. This theme, reformulated by Louis Hartz in his 1955 book *The Liberal Tradition in America*, has long enjoyed an uncontested hegemony, and it is to this characteristic that has been generally attributed the double absence in America of a real conservative tradition and of an important socialist movement. Many people have also seen in this characteristic the secret of the force and vitality of the new world. And yet, for several years now, it appears that the Americans have been more and more critical vis-à-vis this predominance of democratic liberalism: as a result some people have researched other forms of identity and have started to scrutinize their past in order to discover signs of the presence of other traditions.

By the end of the 1960s, a 'neo-conservative' movement was organized to guard against the 'excess of democracy'. Raising the spectre of the 'precipice of equality', this group, composed of prestigious intellectuals united around the reviews *Commentary* and *The Public Interest*, launched an offensive against the democratic wave which the various social movements of this decade represented.[1] They denounced the excess of demands that this multiplication of new rights imposes on the state and the danger that this explosion of egalitarian claims poses to the system of authority. At about the same time, a group of 'neo-liberals' attacked the measure of redistribution within the Great Society and denounced the increasing intervention of the state in the economy. They preached, with Milton Friedman, a return to free market capitalism. For both of these groups, the target is in fact the articulation between liberalism and democracy: the subversive potential of the democratic idea confronting the preservation of the dominant social relations.[2]

Recently, a new voice has been making itself heard: it is no longer democracy that is the target of critique, but liberalism that is held responsible, because of its deep-seated individualism, for the destruction of community values and the progressive deterioration of public life. This type of critique, which has both leftist and conservative variants, is original because it operates within the framework of the rediscovery of a tradition thus far hidden in the United States, that of 'civic republicanism'. This tradition – which some prefer to call 'civic humanism' – affirms in its political discourse that true human realization is only possible when one acts as a citizen of a free and self-governing political community. According to Pocock – one of those who has contributed the most to its reconstruction – the origins of such a conception are to be found in the Aristotelian vision of man as *zoon politikon* (the political animal), in the work of Cicero, and in the Roman ideal of the *res publica* (the public things); but it is in fifteenth-century Florence that it acquires the characteristics which go on to influence Anglo-American political thought of the seventeenth and eighteenth centuries, through the work of James Harrington and the neo-Harringtonians.[3] This is a political language which effects a synthesis between the Aristotelian and Machiavellian elements, where the notions of the 'common good', of 'civic virtue' and of 'corruption' play a central role.

In recent decades, a spectacular reorientation in the interpretation of the American Revolution has occurred which has particularly brought to light the importance of civic republicanism in the revolutionary period. Against the dominant interpretation, which saw in this revolution a rupture of the rationalist type with the old world, influenced principally by the ideas of Locke, the work of historians like Bailyn and Wood[4] has shown that it had been profoundly influenced by the culture of neo-Harringtonian civic humanism; whence arose the central place of the idea of 'corruption' in the political language of American patriots, as disclosed in the analysis of their pamphlets made by Bailyn. It is not until later that the classical conception of politics, in which individuals actively participate in the *res publica*, slips towards a new paradigm: that of representative democracy. According to Gordon Wood, it is the federal constitution of 1787 which marks the end of classical politics and the installation of a new paradigm where the people are no longer conceived as connected by an identity of interests but as 'an agglomeration of hostile individuals coming together for their mutual benefit in the construction of a society'.[5]

It is at that time that insistence on the necessity of public virtue and the common good disappeared, giving place to the new conception of public opinion. Wood shows how a new formula of government made its appearance, one which implied a conception of the political as a compromise between interests whose formulation was exterior to the political action itself. This new conception, which qualifies in general as 'liberal', became dominant during the nineteenth century, but according to some people the republican conception was not completely effaced. Pocock asserts, for example, that it persisted underground thanks to the upholding of premodern and anti-industrial symbols in American culture.[6] It is to this tradition that the authors who criticized liberal individualism will appeal, affirming that it enabled the Americans to retain a certain sense of community which allowed them to resist the corrosive effects of individualism.[7] In the revitalization of this tradition of civic republicanism, they see the solution to the crisis that American society is going through today – a crisis that consists, according to them, in the destruction of the social bond due to the liberal promotion of the individual who only knows how to look after his own interest and who rejects any obligation that could shackle his freedom. Whereas the neoconservatives see in the democratic idea the origin of the difficulties of the system of liberal democracy, it is for the authors called 'communitarians' the disappearance of civic virtue and the identification of a political community where citizenship implies rights but also duties which are central. The latter is a consequence of the increasing privatization of social life and of the disappearance of public space, and this can only be remedied by a restoration of the value of political participation. Today, the liberal illusion that harmony could be born from the free play of private interests, and that modern society no longer needs civic virtue, has finally shown itself to be dangerous; it puts in question the very existence of the democratic process. Whence comes the necessity of a new political culture which reconnects with the tradition of civic republicanism and restores dignity to politics.

A New Liberal Paradigm

It is not surprising that the communitarians of today, like the neoconservatives of yesterday, chose John Rawls as their principal target. In effect, since its publication in 1971, *A Theory of Justice* has been hailed as a magisterial work inaugurating a 'new liberal paradigm'.[8] This 'deontological' or 'rights based' paradigm has put an end to the incontestable supremacy of utilitarianism in Anglo-Saxon theoretical reflection, and all criticism of liberalism must come to grips with what is considered its most advanced elaboration.

The position of Rawls has evolved in a rather substantial manner since the publication of his book,[9] which poses certain problems for grasping the coherence of his theory and judging the criticisms directed at him. *A Theory of Justice* implied that Rawls was looking for an algorithm for rational choice, for an Archimedian point guaranteeing the universal character of his theory of 'fairness'. His problem was to determine which principles of justice free and rational persons would choose, if they were placed in a situation of equality, in order to define the fundamental terms of their association. Afterwards he declared that he only wanted to elaborate a conception of justice for modern democratic societies, by starting from the common intuitions of the members of these societies. His objective was to articulate and to make explicit the ideas and principles latent within our common sense; he therefore would not claim to have formulated a conception of justice that is 'true' but rather proposed the principles that were valid for us, as a function of our history, our traditions, our aspirations and the way we conceive our identity.[10]

Contrary to utilitarianism, Rawls does not conceive of the person as a pure, rational individual exclusively searching for his own well-being, but as a moral person susceptible not only to 'rational' action (understood as instrumental action in one's own interest) but also to what he calls 'reasonable' action, implying moral considerations and a sense of justice in the organization of social cooperation. This is a method he designates by the term 'Kantian constructivism' in order to indicate that he is working with a conception of the person conceived in the Kantian manner as a free and equal moral person.

For a liberal of the Kantian type such as Rawls, who defends a form of liberalism where the right must not depend on any utilitarian conception, it is important that what justifies the right is not the maximization of the general welfare, nor any other particular conception of the good, and that the defence of individual wants has priority in relation to the general welfare. This is why he asserts that the reasonable must have priority over the rational, for the demand of equitable terms of cooperation must limit the boundaries of liberty exercised by individuals in the definition and pursuit of their own interests. This means that there will be 'priority of the right over the good', that is to say, a framework of rights and of fundamental liberties over the different conceptions of good that are permitted to individuals.[11] Rawls considers the aim to be not simply to enlarge the welfare of society as a whole if this implies the sacrifice of a certain number of persons. It is necessary to treat all the individuals as ends in themselves and not as means, a precept that he reproaches utilitarianism for not respecting. For this theory, in effect, individuals are only units of calculation in the maximization of the general interest; in aggregating individuals, it homogenizes them and sacrifices private interests in the name of the utility of the majority. Rawls undertakes to ensure the fundamental rights of individuals and their freedom in a much more complete way than utilitarianism, for this theory of justice is constructed in a manner that respects their plurality and specificity.

But for this agreement over the principles of justice to be truly equitable, it is necessary to find a point of view which is not influenced by the particular circumstances of the participants and their interests. It is this role that Rawls makes the 'original position' play, which, with its veil of ignorance, conceals from participants their exact place in society, their talents, their objectives and all that could be prejudicial to their impartiality. It serves to mediate between the Kantian conception of the person – which Rawls hopes to be able thus to disengage from the metaphysics with which it is weighed down in Kant's work and to redefine in strictly empirical terms – and the principles of justice which he is concerned to construct. The original position designates therefore a heuristic situation of freedom and equality which allows the participants to select, in the procedure of deliberation, the principles of justice for organizing social cooperation between free and equal persons. Therefore there is no independent criterion of justice and it is the very procedure which guarantees that the result produced will be fair. This method of Kantian constructivism leads to the formulation of the following two principles of justice: (1) Everyone has an equal right to the most extensive total system of liberty compatible with an identical liberty for others. (2) Economic and social inequalities must be arranged in such a way that: (a) they give the greatest benefit to the least advantaged (this is the famous difference principle); (b) they are attached to functions and positions open to all under conditions of fair equality of opportunity.

The first principle has priority over the second, and clause (b) has priority over clause (a), so that it is impossible to legitimize any restriction whatsoever of liberty or equality of opportunity with the argument that it contributes to improve the lot of the less well off. Rawls revises the general conception of his theory of justice in the following way: 'all social primary goods – liberty and opportunity, income and wealth, and the bases of self-respect – are to be distributed equally unless an unequal distribution of any or all of these goods is to the advantage of the least favored.'[12]

Rawls considers that his theory of justice at last provides the reply to the question, so controversial, of which principles of justice should organize the terms of social cooperation between free and equal persons. He thinks he has successfully formulated a direct principle which allows the values of liberty and equality to be put to work in social institutions, thereby resolving the conflict that has persisted in democratic thought for two centuries.

Nevertheless, such a pretension has lost no time in being put in question. As early as 1974 Robert Nozick tried to show in *Anarchy, State and Utopia* how, while starting from a similar position to that of Rawls, one could arrive at a diametrically opposed conception of justice. In effect, whereas Rawls is an unquestioned defender of the liberal democratic welfare state, which he means to justify as the most rational and just political form, Nozick is a defender of a minimal state, which limits itself to defend law and order and which entirely eliminates the redistributive function. According to him, social justice does not exist, if by this one means distributive justice, and he declares that a society is just so long as its members possess that which they have a right to, independently of the forms of distribution of wealth this implies.[13]

Liberal Individualism in Question

It is not a question here of analysing the entirety of the debate which the work of Rawls has raised, but of examining the arguments of critics who qualify as 'communitarian'. The target of this critique of Rawls's work and the new paradigm he established is the philosophy of liberalism, on account of its individualism. It denounces the ahistorical, asocial and disembodied conception of the subject that is implied by the idea of an individual endowed with natural rights prior to society, and rejects the thesis of the priority of the right over the good. Against the Kantian inspiration of Rawls, the communitarian authors call upon Aristotle and Hegel: against liberalism they appeal to the tradition of civic republicanism.

For Charles Taylor the liberal view of the subject is 'atomist'[14] because it affirms the self-sufficient character of the individual; it constitutes a real impoverishment in relation to the Aristotelian notion of man as fundamentally a political animal who can only realize his human nature in the bosom of a society. He maintains that this conception lies behind the destruction of public life through the development of bureaucratic individualism. According to Taylor, it is thanks to participation in a community of language and of mutual discourse concerning the just and unjust, the good and the bad, that rationality can develop and that man can become a moral subject capable of discovering the good; therefore there cannot be a priority of the right over the good. While referring particularly to Nozick, he shows the absurdity of claiming to start from the priority of natural rights in order to deduce the entirety of the social context. In effect, this modern individual, with his rights, is the result of a long and complex historical development and it is only in a certain type of society that the existence of such a free individual, capable of choosing his own objectives, is possible.[15]

Alasdair MacIntyre,[16] for his part, reproaches Rawls and Nozick for proposing a conception of justice which does not leave room for the notion, fundamental according to him, of 'virtue'. He attributes this failing to their conception of a society composed of individuals whose interests are defined prior to and independent of the construction of any moral or social bond between them. Now, says MacIntyre, the notion of virtue only has a place in the context of a community whose original bond is a shared understanding as much for the good of man as for the good of the community and where the individuals identify their fundamental interests with reference to these goods.[17] He sees in the rejection of liberalism of all ideas of a 'common good' the source of the nihilism that is slowly destroying our societies.

But it is in the work of Michael Sandel that one finds the most extensive communitarian critique. In *Liberalism and the Limits of Justice*[18] he carries out a precise analysis of Rawls's theory of justice in order to prove its inconsistent character. He attacks principally the thesis of the priority of the right over the good and the conception of the subject this implies. If Rawls affirms that justice is the primordial virtue of social institutions, it is, he says, because his deontological liberalism requires a conception of justice which does not presuppose any particular conception of the good, so as to serve as the framework within which different conceptions of the good would be possible. In the deontological conception, in effect, the primacy of justice is not only described as a moral priority but also as a privileged form of justification. The right is prior to the good not only because its demands have precedence but also because its principles are derived in an independent manner.[19] But for this right to exist prior to the good it would be necessary for the subject to exist independently of his/her intentions and his/her ends. Such a conception requires, therefore, a subject who can have an identity defined prior to the values and objectives that he/she chooses. It is, in effect, the capacity to choose, not the choices that he makes, that defines such a subject. He can never have ends which are constitutive of his identity and this denies him the possibility of participation in a community where it is the very definition of who he is that is in question.[20]

According to Sandel, in Rawls's problematic such a 'constitutive' type of community is unthinkable and community can only be conceived as simple cooperation between individuals whose interests are already given and who join together in order to defend them and to advance them. His central thesis is that this unencumbered conception of the subject, incapable of constitutive engagements, is at the same time necessary so that the right can have priority over the good, and contradictory with the principles of justice which Rawls intends to justify. In effect, the difference principle being a principle of sharing, it presupposes the existence of a moral bond between those who are going to distribute social goods, and therefore of a constitutive community whose recognition it requires. But, Sandel declares, it is precisely such a community that is excluded by the Rawlsian conception of the subject without attachments and who is defined prior to the ends he chooses. In consequence, Rawls's project miscarries, for 'we cannot be persons for whom justice is primary and also be persons for whom the difference principle is a principle of justice.'[21]

Politics of Rights or Politics of the Common Good?

The critique of Sandel is based principally on the position defended by Rawls in *A Theory of Justice* and does not take into account the subsequent evolution of his thought; on a number of points his recent articles modify his conception of the subject in a rather substantial manner.[22] Nevertheless the arguments of Sandel against the disembodied subject found in liberal philosophy are really pertinent and there is a clear contradiction in wanting to found a theory of distributive justice upon the premises of liberal individualism. In this sense liberals like Nozick or Hayek who deny the very existence of such a concept are certainly more coherent.[23] One can only be in agreement with Sandel when he affirms that Rawls does not succeed in justifying the primacy of justice and the priority of the right over the good in a convincing manner. But one cannot follow him when he concludes that this proves the superiority of a politics of the common good over a politics of defending rights.[24] The fact that the argumentation of Rawls is inadequate does not imply that his objective must be rejected.

This question of the priority of the right over the good constitutes the essence of the debate and it permits us to demonstrate the limits of the liberal conception as much as the ambiguities of the communitarian critique and its dangers. As Sandel has remarked, for the liberals of the Kantian type such as Rawls, the priority of the right over the good means not only that one cannot sacrifice individual rights in the name of the general good, but also that the principles of justice cannot be derived from a particular conception of the good life.[25] This is the cardinal principle of liberalism, according to which there cannot be a sole conception of *eudaimonia*, of happiness, which is capable of being imposed on all, but that each one must have the possibility of discovering his happiness as he understands it, to fix for himself his own proper objectives and to attempt to realize them in his own way. The communitarians, for their part, affirm that one cannot define the right prior to the good, for it is only through our participation in a community which defines the good that we can have a sense of the right and a conception of justice. Here we have an irreproachable argument, which, however, does not authorize Sandel's conclusion that we must reject the priority of justice as the principal virtue of social institutions as well as the defence of individual rights and return to a politics based on a common moral order. Such a conclusion rests, in effect, on a fundamental equivocation concerning the very notion of the common good, which is in great part due to Rawls himself. Until recently,[26] he insisted that his theory of justice belonged to moral philosophy. But the latter refers, of course, not to morality but to the political and requires distinguishing between the 'common moral good' and the 'common political good'. Once such a distinction has been established, the consequences that Sandel draws out of the epistemological incoherences of Rawls appear unacceptable.

Let us examine this a little more closely. Rawls wants to defend the liberal pluralism that requires not imposing upon man a conception of well-being and a particular plan of life. Individual morality is for liberals a private question and each one must be able to organize his life as he intends. Whence the importance of rights and the fact that the principles of justice cannot privilege a particular conception of well-being. But it is evident that this priority of the right over the good is only possible in a certain type of society with determinate institutions, and there cannot be an absolute priority of the right over the good since – as the communitarians assert with reason – it is only within a specific community, defining itself by the good that it postulates, that an individual with his rights can exist. But it would be necessary to specify that it is a question of *political* community, that is to say, of a *regime* (in the Greek sense of *politeia*) which is defined by the political good that it puts to work.[27] Certain regimes characterize themselves by the fact that they make no distinction between the good of man and the good of the city, but the separation of these two spheres by modernity and the rejection of a single conception of the moral good should not ignore the existence of the 'political good', the good which defines a political association as such. Therefore if a liberal democratic regime must be agnostic in terms of morality, it is not – and cannot be – agnostic concerning the political good since it affirms the political principles of liberty and equality. It is only within such a regime and as a function of the political good which defines it that the priority of rights with respect to the different conceptions of the moral good is possible. If the communitarians are therefore authorized to put in question the priority of the right over the good as it appears in the work of Rawls, it is nevertheless illegitimate on their part to claim, as Sandel does, that this requires abandoning liberal pluralism as well as a politics based on rights, since such a priority is precisely what characterizes a liberal democratic regime.

Morality and Politics

It is obvious that what is really in question is the status of the political, and this discussion reveals our present-day incapacity for considering the political in a modern manner, that is to say, in a manner which is not simply instrumental – which implies taking into account all that is involved in the idea of a 'political good', of the ethic proper to politics – but all the while respecting the modern separation between morality and politics. Neither Rawls nor Sandel is capable of considering this distinction adequately, though for different reasons. In the case of Sandel, his critique of liberalism operates within a fundamental Aristotelian problematic where there is not yet a separation between morality and politics and where there is no true differentiation between 'the common political good' and 'the common moral good'. In the ancient conception the political was in fact subordinate to the ethical, and it is this which explains the tendency of certain communitarian critics influenced by Aristotle, like Sandel or MacIntyre, to believe that in order to govern in terms of the common good it is necessary to encourage a singular moral vision and to reject liberal pluralism. Whence their generally negative attitude in relation to modernity and their nostalgia for an original community of the *Gemeinschaft* type. As for Rawls, his incapacity to consider the political is explained by the fact that this constitutes the blind spot of liberalism, which tends to reduce it to an instrumental activity. In effect, all the normative aspects proper to political philosophy have been discredited by the development of political science and the positivist distinction between fact and value. It is thus that an entire series of questions which are incontestably of a political nature, such as the question of justice, have been relegated to the domain of morals, and this is without doubt why Rawls has for so long stubbornly presented his theory of justice as a contribution to moral philosophy.

This incapacity of liberalism to think of the political has deep roots. As Carl Schmitt has pointed out, the pure and rigorous principle of liberalism cannot give birth to a specifically political conception.[28] Every consistent individualism must indeed negate the political, since it requires that the individual remains *terminus a quo* and *terminus ad quem*. This is why, according to Schmitt, liberal thought moves in a polarity between ethics and economics, and restricts itself to wanting to impose ethical obligations on the political or to submit it to the economic. Whence the fact that there is no genuine liberal politics but only a liberal critique of politics in the name of the defence of individual liberty.[29]

It is because this liberal individualism does not allow conceiving of the collective aspect of social life as being constitutive that there is – as the communitarians indicate – a contradiction at the heart of Rawls's project. His ambition of rationally founding the requirements of equality present in the common sense of Western democracies, starting from an individualist conception of the subject, can only run aground. And this fundamental limitation of liberalism cannot be resolved by recourse to morality. The appeal to Rawls of the Kantian conception of the moral person and the introduction of the reasonable next to the rational permit him to establish moral limits to the pursuit of private egoism but without truly putting into question the individualist conception. It is only in the context of a tradition that really makes room for the political dimension of human existence, and which permits thinking of citizenship other than as the simple possession of rights, that one can give an account of democratic values. This critique of liberalism must nevertheless operate in the framework of modernity and of the conquests of the democratic revolution. While still having much to teach us, the classical conception is no longer applicable. The emergence of the individual, the separation of Church and State, the principle of religious tolerance, the development of civil society – all these elements have led us to distinguish the domain of morality from that of politics. If it is important to pose once again the question of the common good and that of civic virtue, this must be done in a modern fashion, without postulating a single moral good. We should not forego the gains of liberalism, and the critique of individualism implies neither the abandonment of the notion of 'rights' nor that of pluralism.

Justice and Pluralism

Such is the approach of Michael Walzer who, although he puts himself on the side of the communitarians, is not opposed to the political ideals of liberalism. On the contrary, his project is to defend and to radicalize the liberal democratic tradition.[30] Walzer is opposed to the type of philosophical reasoning which assumes that a thinker detaches himself from all ties with his community in order to discover allegedly universal and eternal truths.[31] According to him, the philosopher must stay in the cave to assume fully his status as a member of a particular community; and his role consists in interpreting for its citizens the world of meanings they have in common. If he denounces the rationalism and the universalism of the Enlightenment and proposes re-evaluating concepts such as those of tradition and community, it is in order to defend the democratic ideal in a more effective manner.

Though critical of the epistemological position of Rawls, he is nevertheless in agreement with the latter concerning the priority of justice and the idea that in our societies this consists in the institutionalization of liberty and equality. But Walzer distinguishes himself from Rawls in the way in which he conceives of equality, and in *Spheres of Justice* he presents a pluralistic theory of social justice whose goal is the realization of what he calls a 'complex equality'. This is, according to him, the only conception of equality adapted to modern societies, where the degree of differentiation is very elaborate.[32] He considers, in effect, that we conceive equality too often in the mode of simple equality which tends to render people as equal as possible in their global situation. Such a view necessarily implies the constant intervention of the state in order to prevent the emergence of all forms of domination. Therefore this view opens the way toward totalitarianism, which pretends to coordinate systematically the distribution of all goods in all spheres. This is why Walzer affirms that if one wants to make equality a central objective of politics, and also respect liberty, one can only conceive of it as complex equality. This requires that different social goods be distributed, not in a uniform manner but in terms of a diversity of criteria which reflect the diversity of those social goods and the meanings attached to them. Equality is a complex relationship between persons mediated by a series of social goods; it does not consist in an identity of possession.[33] The important thing is not to violate the principles of distribution proper to each sphere and to avoid success in one sphere implying the possibility of exercising preponderance in others, as is now the case with wealth. He cites Pascal: 'Tyranny is the wish to obtain by one means what can only be had by another. We owe different duties to different qualities: love is the proper response to charm, fear to strength, and belief to learning.'[34] Justice is not, therefore, only a question of interpretation and application of the criteria of distribution, but also the distinctions and the boundaries between the different spheres. It is essential that no social good be used as the means of domination and that concentration of political power, wealth, honour, and especially desirable office, in the same hands be avoided.

The interest of the perspective adopted by Walzer is that it permits the critique of liberal individualism and its epistemological presuppositions while conserving and even enriching the contribution of pluralism. It also demonstrates how one can imagine justice without searching for a universal point of view and without elaborating general principles valid for all societies. For Walzer, it is only by starting from a specific political community, within the tradition which constitutes it and the social meanings common to its members, that the question of justice can be posed. It does not make sense, according to him, to declare that a society of the hierarchical type is unjust because the distribution of social goods is not brought about according to egalitarian principles. If equality is a central objective for us, it is because we live in a liberal democratic society where the institutions and social meanings are profoundly impregnated by this value, which renders possible its utilization as a criterion for judging the just and unjust. In so far as political principles – equality as well as liberty – are susceptible to a number of interpretations, there cannot be definitive agreement upon the definition of liberty and equality, the social relations where these principles must be put to work, or their mode of institutionalization. Different political philosophies offer different interpretations, but it is because these values are central to our tradition that such a discussion is possible and that we pose the problem of justice in these terms.

Aristotle or Machiavelli?

To the liberal conception of the individual, the communitarian authors oppose the image of the citizen found in the tradition of civic republicanism. Contrary to liberalism, this tradition furnishes a language which permits thinking of the political in a noninstrumental way. It played an important role in American political culture of the eighteenth century and has not completely disappeared; the communitarians propose to revive it, thus providing Americans with the capacity to articulate their experience and to conceive of their identity in terms of active participation in a political community. It is in a re-evaluation of the political sphere and in a rehabilitation of the notion of 'civic virtue' that they see the solution to the legitimation crisis which affects the democratic system.[35]

The problem resides in the ambiguity of the notion of 'civic humanism' or 'civic republicanism' as it has been recently elaborated. This *mélange* of Aristotelian and Machiavellian elements can in effect give rise to extremely different interpretations, according to whether one accepts with Aristotle the unity of the good and the indivisibility of ethics and politics, or, following Machiavelli, distinguishes these two domains and insists upon the central role of conflict in the preservation of liberty. I have already indicated how, in the work of authors like Sandel or MacIntyre, the critique of liberalism ignores the characteristics of modern democracy and leads to a rejection of modernity. This is not a necessary consequence of the communitarian position and it is not the case with Walzer or Taylor, who both endeavour to integrate certain achievements of liberalism; it is not therefore an intrinsically antimodern problematic as certain liberals suggest.[36]

But in the absence of the elaboration of a republican model adequate to the requirements of modern democracies, the current attraction for civic republicanism can only give rise to a confusion with possibly dangerous consequences for all those who defend the extension of rights and democratic practices. It is fundamental to distinguish between 'civic conscience' – that is to say, the requirements proper for all citizens of a liberal democratic regime where the criteria of justice are those of liberty and equality – and a postulated substantive common good which would impose on all a singular conception of *eudaimonia*. Civic conscience does not imply that there must necessarily be consensus, and the republican ideal does not require the suppression of diversity in favour of unity. A republican conception which draws inspiration from Machiavelli, but also from Montesquieu, Tocqueville and Mill, can make room for that which constitutes the central contribution of liberalism: the separation of public and private and the defence of pluralism. But this requires thinking of citizenship in a democratic fashion, that is to say without renouncing individual liberty. Such a task is only possible if we strive to conceptualize liberty other than as the defence of individual rights against the state, while taking care not to sacrifice the individual to the citizen.[36]

Liberty of the Ancients or Liberty of the Moderns?

The work inspired by the 'new history' pioneered by Quentin Skinner is particularly pertinent to such a project. In an article where he analyses the results of this type of research, Pocock indicates how in the origin of modern political thought we find two styles of political language, one of which will succeed in imposing itself to the detriment of the other.[37] There is on the one hand the language of virtue, which is that of classical republicanism, and on the other the language of rights, which expresses the paradigm of natural right and is found in jurisprudence. The term *libertas* is present in the two languages but with a different meaning. In the language of the jurists, *libertas* has the meaning of *imperium*, the freedom to carry out their own laws. The liberty of the citizen consists therefore in the freedom to go about one's business under the protection of the law. In republican language, on the contrary, one insists upon liberty in the sense of participation in the government of the state, tied to a conception of man as a political animal who only realizes his nature through his activities in the public domain. These two forms coexisted for a period, and Skinner has shown, in the first volume of *The Foundations of Modern Political Thought*,[38] how the Italian republics' struggle for independence was simultaneously conducted in the republican language and in that of the jurists. Afterwards the language of natural right supplants that of virtue, but coterminous with the tradition of liberalism, centred on law and right, there was during the beginning of the modern period a tradition of republican humanism where the personality was conceived in terms of virtue. It is only with Hobbes that the mode of individualist political reasoning, in which liberty limits itself to the defence of individual rights, becomes dominant.

The objective of Skinner in his most recent work[39] is to re-evaluate the republican conception which, during the Renaissance in Europe, had reformulated the classical Roman conception of the citizen, because he believes that it can provide us with a conception of liberty more adequate than the liberal conception. He is fully conscious of the problem posed today by the relation between individual liberty and political liberty. Since Benjamin Constant, in effect, it has generally been admitted that the 'liberty of the moderns' consists in the peaceful enjoyment of private independence and that this implies the renunciation of the 'liberty of the ancients', the active participation in collective power, because this leads to a subordination of the individual to the community.

This same thesis has been reformulated in a celebrated article by Isaiah Berlin,[40] who distinguished between the 'negative' conception of liberty, known simply as the absence of coercion, and which requires that a part of human existence remains independent of the sphere of social control, and the 'positive' conception of liberty, which stems from the desire of the individual to be his own master and implies the idea of the realization and accomplishment of a true human nature. According to Berlin, this second conception is potentially totalitarian and unacceptable for a liberal, and he concludes from this that the idea of democracy and of self-government cannot belong to the liberal idea of liberty. He asserts that the entire positive conception of liberty is antimodern because it requires postulation of the existence of an objective notion of the good life for man. Thus, all those who defend the republican conception of liberty, the idea of *libertas*, that liberty can be assured only in a community which is self-governing, appear as the adversaries of modernity.

Skinner rejects this thesis and attempts to prove that one can find in the civic republican tradition, and more particularly in the work of Machiavelli, a conception of liberty that, while negative – for it does not imply the objective notion of *eudiamonia* – still includes the ideals of political participation and civic virtue. It is thus in the *Discorsi* that Machiavelli proposes a conception of liberty as the capacity of men to pursue their proper objectives, their *humori*, all the while affirming that in order to secure the necessary conditions for avoiding coercion and servitude, which would render impossible the exercise of this individual liberty, it is indispensable that men fulfil certain public functions and cultivate the requisite virtues. If it is necessary to practise civic virtue and to serve the common good, it is so, for Machiavelli, in order for us to guarantee the degree of personal liberty which will permit us to pursue our ends.[41]

Such a line of argument certainly requires further development, but it indicates an extremely fruitful path. The principal task of a modern and democratic political philosophy is precisely the articulation of individual liberty and political liberty, for it is there that the question of pluralistic and democratic citizenship is rooted. It is the great merit of Skinner to show a path back to Machiavelli. The latter incontestably represents a fundamental point of reference for those who want to think politically today, and if it is important to renew intimacy with the tradition of civic republicanism, it is essential that it be under his aegis. The communitarian critique of liberalism can thus lead us to rediscover a way of thinking that was first developed several centuries ago but whose potentialities have not yet been exploited, for reflection upon the political was, with Hobbes, to take a so-called scientific direction, implying the rejection of its normative aspects and the predominance of an instrumental conception.

Translated by William Falcetano

Notes

1. One finds, for example, Irving Kristol, Daniel Patrick Moynihan, Daniel Bell, Samuel Huntington and Zbigniew Brezinski, to cite only the most well known. For an

excellent analysis of this movement one can consult the book of Peter Steinfels, *The Neo-Conservatives*, New York 1979.

2. On this offensive, as much of the neoliberals as of the neoconservatives, against democracy, we return to our article 'Democracy and the New Right', *Politics and Power*, pp. 221–35, in 4, London 1979.

3. J. G. A. Pocock, *The Machiavellian Moment: Florentine Political Thought and The Atlantic Republican Tradition*, Princeton 1975, *Politics, Language and Time*, New York 1973, and *Virtue, Commerce and History*, Cambridge 1985. It is necessary, however, to specify that Pocock himself is not one of those who proposes to revive the tradition of civic republicanism today.

4. Bernard Bailyn, *The Ideological Origins of the American Revolution*, Cambridge, Mass. 1967, and *The Origins of American Politics*, New York 1967; Gordon S. Wood, *The Creation of the American Republic 1776–1787*, Chapel Hill 1969.

5. Wood, *The Creation of the American Republic*, p. 607.

6. Pocock, *The Machiavellian Moment*, p. 549.

7. This is the thesis defended by Robert Bellah and his collaborators in *Habits of the Heart, Individualism and Commitment in American Life*, Berkeley 1985, just as by William M. Sullivan in *Reconstructing Public Philosophy*, Berkeley 1982.

8. John Rawls, *A Theory of Justice*, Cambridge, Mass. 1971.

9. Two articles particularly render manifest this evolution of Rawls: 'Kantian Constructivism in Moral Theory', *The Journal of Philosophy*, vol. LXXVII, no. 9, September 1980, and 'Justice as Fairness: Political not Metaphysical', *Philosophy and Public Affairs*, vol. 14, no. 3, Summer 1985.

10. Rawls, 'Kantian Constructivism', pp. 516–19.

11. Rawls, *A Theory of Justice*, pp. 446–52.

12. Ibid., pp. 302–3.

13. Robert Nozick, *Anarchy, State and Utopia*, New York 1974, ch. 7.

14. Charles Taylor, *Philosophy and the Human Sciences*, Philosophical Papers 2, Cambridge 1985, ch. 7, 'Atomism'.

15. Taylor, *Philosophy and the Human Sciences*, p. 200.

16. Alasdair MacIntyre, *After Virtue*, Notre Dame 1984.

17. Ibid., p. 256.

18. Michael J. Sandel, *Liberalism and the Limits of Justice*, Cambridge 1982.

19. Ibid., p. 15.

20. Ibid., p. 150.

21. Ibid., p. 178.

22. Rawls now puts more and more stress on the role played in his theory by the Kantian conception of the moral person. This indicates that certain moral principles are inscribed in the original position itself and that it is no longer a question of a pure theory of rational choice.

23. Friedrich A. Hayek, *Law, Legislation and Liberty*, Volume 2, Chicago 1976, p. 69; Nozick, *Anarchy, State and Utopia*.

24. Michael J. Sandel, 'Morality and the Liberal Ideal', *New Republic*, 7 May 1984, p. 166.

25. Sandel, *Liberalism and the Limits of Justice*, p. 156.

26. Rawls, 'Justice as Fairness: Political not Metaphysical', p. 224, where in note 2 he reconsiders his conception of justice as political and not moral.

27. We can still accept the Aristotelian definition of the political community as an association which aims at the good of all. But this must today be comprised in exclusively political terms as constituted by the political principles of an association, and this does not require the existence of a single conception of the moral good. It is therefore the ethics appropriate to politics that is the task of a modern political philosophy.

28. Carl Schmitt, *The Concept of the Political*, Rutgers 1971, p. 70.

29. Schmitt, p. 71. To reconsider the pertinence of the critique of liberalism made by Schmitt evidently does not imply that one must accept his position in its totality.

30. Among the numerous books of Michael Walzer, those which touch more on the subject treated here are the following: *Obligations. Essays on Disobedience, War and*

Citizenship, Cambridge, Mass. 1970, *Radical Principles: Reflections of an Unreconstructed Democrat*, New York 1980, and especially *Spheres of Justice, A Defence of Pluralism and Equality*, New York 1983.

31. Walzer, *Spheres of Justice*, p. xiv, and his article 'Philosophy and Democracy', *Political Theory*, vol. 9, no. 3, August 1981, where he presented his position on this subject in a more detailed manner.

32. Walzer, *Spheres of Justice*, p. 316.

33. Ibid., p. 18.

34. Pascal, *Pensées*; this text is cited in *Spheres of Justice*, p. 18.

35. One can say the same about the position of Hannah Arendt, whose thought inscribes her also within the tradition of civic republicanism.

36. See, for example, H. Hirsch, 'The Theory of Liberalism', and D. Herzog, 'Some Questions for Republicans', both in *Political Theory*, vol. 14, no. 3, August 1986.

37. Pocock, *Virtue, Commerce and History*, ch. 2.

38. Quentin Skinner, *The Foundations of Modern Political Thought*, 2 vols, Cambridge 1978.

39. Quentin Skinner, 'The Idea of Negative Liberty: Philosophical and Historical Perspectives', in R. Rorty, J. B. Schneewind and Q. Skinner, *Philosophy in History*, Cambridge 1984.

40. Isaiah Berlin, 'Two Concepts of Liberty', in *Four Essays on Liberty*, Oxford 1969.

41. Skinner, 'The Idea of Negative Liberty', pp. 217–19.

3

Rawls: Political Philosophy without Politics

Is it possible to disentangle political liberalism from the vocabulary that it has inherited from the rationalism of the Enlightenment on the one hand and from the connotations it has acquired by its long association with economic liberalism on the other? This is, I believe, a crucial question for the elaboration of a modern democratic political philosophy. Several recent debates attest to the need for such an elucidation by forcing us into unacceptable dichotomies. It is particularly evident in the current controversy about modernity and postmodernity and the confrontation between the defenders of the Enlightenment and its detractors. As Richard Rorty pointed out in 'Habermas and Lyotard on Postmodernity': 'We find French critics of Habermas ready to abandon liberal politics in order to avoid universalistic philosophy, and Habermas trying to hang on to universalistic philosophy, with all its problems, in order to support liberal politics.'[1] A very similar confusion is happening among the communitarian critics of liberalism, with several of them failing to distinguish between liberal individualism as a specific doctrine concerning the nature of the human subject, and political liberalism as a set of institutions characteristic of the 'law state': defence of rights, recognition of pluralism, limitation of the role of the state, separation of powers, and so on. Thus communitarians like Sandel and MacIntyre, who refuse the atomist conception of man of liberal individualism, think it necessary to denounce the 'rhetoric of rights and pluralism' and end up by rejecting political liberalism. Even Rorty is guilty of illegitimate amalgamation when he makes bourgeois economic relations an intrinsic component of liberalism. Indeed, his concept of 'liberalism' is extremely ambiguous; if he rightly separates – following Blumenberg – the two aspects of the Enlightenment, that of 'self-assertion' (which can be identified with the political project),[2] and that of 'self-foundation' (the epistemological project), he nevertheless later identifies the political project of modernity with a vague concept of 'liberalism' which includes both capitalism and democracy. His 'postmodernist bourgeois liberalism' is therefore a pure and simple apology for the 'institutions and practices of the rich North Atlantic democracies'[3] that leaves no room for democratic critique.

All those false dilemmas are the result of the conflation under the term 'liberalism' of a series of different discourses which have been articulated together in certain circumstances but that have no necessary relation. First, it is important in order to understand political modernity to distinguish two traditions, liberal and democratic, which were only articulated in the nineteenth century. Then, one must not confuse this 'political modernity' with the process of modernization carried out under the domination of capitalist relations of production. Some liberals of course argue that there cannot be political liberalism without economic liberalism and a free market economy, but that is only the expression of one trend within liberalism. Finally, there are a series of philosophical discourses concerning the idea of man, the criteria of rationality, the nature of morality, and so on; they are sometimes referred to as 'the philosophy of liberalism' but are extremely heterogeneous and include positions as different as Kantianism and utilitarianism. It is therefore a mistake to see them as constituting a single doctrine. Many possible articulations can take place between those different 'forms' of liberalism and I want to argue that the acceptance of political liberalism does not require us to endorse either individualism or economic liberalism, nor does it commit us to a defence of universalism and rationalism. I will take the case of Rawls's deontological liberalism as an example of those multiple articulations and use it as a starting point to discuss the nature and the role of political philosophy in a democratic society.

Rawls's Theory of Justice

Rawls's work is a good illustration of the point I am making. First, we have here a defence of political liberalism which establishes its autonomy from economic liberalism. As Brian Barry indicated, the significance of *A Theory of Justice* is that it is 'a statement of liberalism which isolates its crucial features by making private property, in the means of production, distribution and exchange, a contingent matter rather than an essential part of the doctrine and introduces a principle of distribution which could, suitably interpreted and with certain factual assumptions, have egalitarian implications.'[4] Moreover, it is an attempt to provide an alternative to utilitarian thought whose

hegemony among liberal moral philosophy had been solidly established. Finally, and this is the aspect I want to examine, Rawls has been
moving away from a universalistic framework and is now stressing the
'situated' character of his theory of justice.

Indeed Rawls pretends that he was misunderstood and that even in
his book he did not intend to pose the question of justice in an
ahistorical manner. But by stating that the principles of justice as
fairness 'are the principles that free and rational persons concerned to
further their own interests would accept in an initial position of
equality as defining the fundamental terms of their association'[5]
without further historical specifications, he was leaving the door wide
open for universalistic types of interpretations. It is only later that he
has specified that his aim was not to elaborate a conception of justice
suitable for all types of societies regardless of their particular social or
historical circumstances but only 'to settle a fundamental disagreement over the just form of social institutions within a democratic
society under modern conditions'.[6] He was therefore trying to find a
solution to the disputed question of how basic social institutions
should be arranged in order to embody the principles of equality and
liberty and how those two ideals should be understood and balanced.
Now, he also emphasizes that the task of articulating a public
conception of justice is primarily a practical social task, not an
epistemological one, and that 'what justifies a conception of justice is
not its being true to an order antecedent and given to us, but its
congruence with a deeper understanding of ourselves and our
aspirations, and our realization that, given our history and the
tradition embedded in our public life, it is the most reasonable doctrine
for us.'[7] After having been one of the main targets of the advocates of
contextualism, has Rawls become one of their champions? Has he
abandoned Dworkin for Rorty? What are today the points of
contention with his communitarian critics? More generally, how
successful is Rawls's 'historicized' version of justice as fairness?

In order to elucidate some of these problems it is necessary to
recapitulate briefly the main ideas of Rawls's theory as they are
presented in a series of articles posterior to *A Theory of Justice*. There he
declares that the aim of political philosophy in a constitutional
democracy is to propose 'a political conception of justice that can not
only provide a fair public basis for the justification of political social and
economic institutions but also help ensure stability from one
generation to the next.'[8] What is at stake is the creation of social unity.
In a democratic society it cannot rest on a shared conception of the
meaning, value and purpose of life; nor can it rest exclusively on a
convergence of self- or group-interest because such a basis of

justification would not be stable enough. Social unity should therefore be secured by an overlapping consensus on a reasonable political conception of justice.

Concerning the nature of such a political conception of justice, Rawls indicates that it is a moral conception worked out for political, social and economic institutions and should not be understood as an application to the political order of a general and comprehensive moral conception. This is to respect the existence of a pluralism that must allow for a plurality of conflicting and incommensurable conceptions of the good. Therefore a political conception of justice must be independent of controversial philosophical and religious doctrines, and no general moral conception can provide a publicly recognized basis for a conception of justice in a modern democratic society. Such a conception can only be formulated in terms of certain fundamental intuitive ideas latent in its common sense and embedded in its institutions.[9]

For that reason, justice as fairness starts with what Rawls considers to be the central intuitive idea implicit in the public culture of a democracy: a view of society as a fair system of cooperation between free and equal persons. The fundamental question of political justice is then to find 'the most appropriate principles for realizing liberty and equality once society is viewed as a system of cooperation between free and equal persons.'[10] Rawls's proposal is to see those principles as the result of an agreement among the people concerned in the light of their mutual advantage. He believes that the idea of a rational self-interested choice can provide a shared idea of citizens' good appropriate for political purposes and independent of any particular doctrine. But such a choice is nevertheless subject to a series of constraints and the original position is introduced in order to specify the conditions of liberty and equality necessary for the agreement to be reached in a fair way. Its 'veil of ignorance' serves to eliminate the bargaining advantages that could affect the process of decision and distort the result. Rawls asserts that once the citizens see themselves as free and equal persons they should recognize that to pursue their own different conceptions of the good they need the same primary goods, that is, the same basic rights, liberties and opportunities as well as the same all-purpose means such as income and wealth and the same social bases of self-respect. They would in consequence agree on a political conception of justice that will state that 'all social primary goods – liberty and opportunity, income and wealth, and the bases of self-respect – are to be distributed equally unless an unequal distribution of any or all of these goods is to the advantage of the least favored.'[11] Such is precisely the general conception behind the two principles of justice specified by Justice as Fairness, the first one requiring that each person is to have an equal right to the most extensive basic liberty, compatible with a similar liberty for others; and the second that goods should only be distributed unequally when that unequal distribution is (a) to the greatest benefit of the least advantaged and (b) attached to offices and positions open to all under conditions of fair opportunity.[12]

The main point of difference with *A Theory of Justice* is the new emphasis put on the fact that the basic ideas of Justice as Fairness are regarded as implicit or latent in the public culture of a democratic society, and the consequent abandonment of the description of the theory of justice as part of the theory of rational choice. Rawls recognizes that this was a mistake and declares: 'What I should have said is that the conception of justice as fairness uses an account of rational choice subject to reasonable conditions to characterize the deliberations of the parties as representatives of free and equal persons . . . There is no thought of trying to derive the content of justice within a framework that uses an idea of the rational as the sole normative idea.'[13] Rawls also stresses that the conception of the person found in the original position is a political conception, a conception of citizens concerned with our public identity, and that it does not presuppose any specific comprehensive view of the nature of the self.

Priority of the Right over the Good

One of the characteristic features of Justice as Fairness is that it affirms the priority of the right over the good. Such a priority indicates that individual rights cannot be sacrificed for the sake of the general welfare, as is the case with utilitarianism, and that the principles of justice impose restrictions on what are the permissible conceptions of their good that individuals are allowed to pursue. This is of course why the principles of justice must be derived independently of any particular conception of the good, since they need to respect the existence of a plurality of competing conceptions of the good in order to be accepted by all citizens. Rawls believes that the superiority of the deontological approach over the teleological one (which asserts the priority of the good and defines the right as what maximizes the good) is that it is the only one providing an adequate representation of the distinctness of individuals and a defence of their inalienable rights. Hence his claim that Justice as Fairness is the theory of justice best suited to a modern democracy.

I think that Rawls is right in arguing that in a modern democracy the principles of justice must be derived independently of any moral, religious or philosophical conception and serve as a framework to determine which particular conceptions of the good are acceptable. But he is defending this thesis in a way that is inadequate and that has left him vulnerable to the communitarian critique. The communitarians object that such a priority of the right cannot exist, because it is only in a specific type of society, with certain institutions, that an individual with rights can exist, and that it is only through our participation in a community which defines the good in a certain way that we can acquire a sense of the right and a conception of justice. As Charles Taylor correctly points out, 'The basic error of atomism in all its forms is that it fails to take account of the degree to which the free individual with his own goals and aspirations, whose just rewards it is trying to protect, is himself only possible within a certain kind of civilization; that it took a long development of certain institutions and practices, of the rule of law, of rules of equal respect, of habits of common deliberation, of common association, of cultural development, and so on, to produce the modern individual.'[14] Once it is recognized that the existence of rights and a conception of justice cannot exist prior to and independently of specific forms of political association – which by definition imply a conception of the good – it becomes obvious that there can never be an absolute priority of the right over the good.

Does that mean that we should therefore reject Rawls's concerns with the priority of justice and the defence of individual rights and come back to a politics of the common good based on shared moral values, as Michael Sandel argues?[15] We find here a dangerous confusion, which accounts for other ambiguity of the communitarian critique and which leads, in authors like Sandel, to the rejection of political liberalism and a denial of pluralism. Its origin resides in the problematic notion of the 'common good' and its implications for the relationship between ethics and politics. Before the advent of modernity, the community was organized around a single idea of a substantive common good and no real distinction existed between ethics and politics, with politics being subordinated to the common good. With the emergence of the individual, the separation between Church and State, the principle of religious toleration, and the development of civil society, a separation took place between politics and what became the sphere of morality. Moral and religious beliefs are now a private matter on which the state cannot legislate and pluralism is a crucial feature of modern democracy, the kind of democracy that is characterized by the absence of a substantive common good.

But if Rawls is right in wanting to defend pluralism and individual rights, he is wrong in believing that such a project requires the rejection of any possible idea of a common good. Because that priority of right he advocates can only exist within the context of a specific political association defined by an idea of the common good; except that in this case it must be understood in strictly political terms, as the political common good of a liberal democratic regime, that is, the principles of the liberal democratic regime qua political association – equality and liberty. There is no need, on the other hand, to reject pluralism and the priority of justice in order to adopt a communitarian approach stressing the character of man as a political and social being whose identity is created within a community of language, meanings and practices. In using the inadequacy in Rawls's formulation to criticize a politics of rights, Sandel is therefore drawing illegitimate conclusions, and a communitarian defence of political liberalism is perfectly possible. Indeed Rawls has been moving in that direction since he acknowledged that his conception of justice is a political one that concerns us qua citizens of a constitutional democracy whose latent ideals it tries to reflect and develop.

Nevertheless his current position is not very consistent and he stands in an awkward position between Kant and Hegel, as Glaston has correctly pointed out. He still maintains the priority of the right but his new emphasis on the conception of the moral person undermines such a priority, since 'if justice is desirable because it aims at our good as moral persons, then justice as fairness rests on a specific conception of the good, from which the "constraints" of right and justice are ultimately derived.'[16] Glaston argues that Rawls's revised theory is difficult to distinguish from the perfectionism that he continues to reject. 'Clearly the ideal of the person functions as a moral goal, in two respects. Individuals choosing principles of justice will seek, first and foremost, to create circumstances in which they can realize and express their moral powers. Second, we as observers will appraise social institutions in light of their propensity to promote the realization and facilitate the expression of these powers, and this standard will take priority over our other concerns.'[17]

I agree with Glaston that Rawls's position today is untenable, though I do not think that the solution consists in assuming openly a perfectionist view but rather, as I shall try to show later, in establishing the conditions that would enable him to base his political conception of justice on strictly political grounds. That will require us to recognize that a liberal democratic regime, if it must be agnostic in terms of morality and religion, cannot be agnostic concerning political values, since by definition it asserts the principles that constitute its specificity qua political association, that is, the political principles of equality and liberty.

Unfortunately too many liberals want to identify political liberalism with the neutral state and do not understand that it is a mistaken and self-defeating strategy. Some like Charles Larmore even argue that the task of liberal theory is to provide a neutral justification of the neutrality of the state.[18] This can only reinforce a tendency, already too much present in liberalism, to transform political problems into administrative and technical ones, and it chimes with theories of neo-conservatives like Niklas Luhmann who want to restrict the field of democratic decisions by turning more and more areas over to the control of supposedly neutral experts.

To be sure, Rawls does not endorse those claims to neutrality and, as we have seen, his theory of justice is getting increasingly loaded with values. By subordinating the rational to the reasonable,[19] he has drastically limited the field of exercise of the rational choice approach. The original position no longer expresses a point of view of neutrality but reflects the ideals implicit in the public culture of a democratic society, and the parties in their deliberation are now guided by the exercise and development of their two moral powers. Moreover, Rawls insists that the aim of a theory of justice is not to create merely a *modus vivendi* but an overlapping consensus on shared principles of justice that imply the realization of political values. He wants to steer a course 'between the Hobbesian strand in liberalism – liberalism as a *modus vivendi* secured by a convergence of self- and group-interests as coordinated and balanced by well-designed constitutional arrangements – and a liberalism founded on a comprehensive moral doctrine such as that of Kant or Mill'.[20]

Justice and the Political

Despite the fact that I sympathize with Rawls's assertion that we should start from our democratic tradition to elaborate a conception of justice instead of searching for a point of view exterior to our historical insertion in order to reach supposedly 'true' ahistorical principles, I consider his approach inadequate. The reason lies, I believe, in the unsatisfactory notion of the political that we find in his work. As far as politics is present at all in Rawls, it is reduced to the 'politics of interest', that is, the pursuit of differing interests defined prior to and independently of their possible articulation by competing alternative discourses. The aim of his theory of justice is to regulate that pursuit by establishing agreed-upon, neutral rules. Of course those rules have for Rawls a moral character, so his conception is not a purely instrumental one; there should be moral limits imposed on the search for self-interest. But between the 'reasonable' and the 'rational' there is no space left for something properly political, whose nature we could establish independently of morality or economics. The term might be present – and increasingly so – in his writings but only in some kind of negative way to specify a form of morality which is not based on a comprehensive doctrine and that applies only to certain areas.

We are told that 'the first feature of a political conception of justice is that, while such a conception is, of course, a moral conception, it is a moral conception worked out for a specific kind of subject, namely, for political, social and economic institutions' and that 'the second feature complements the first: a political conception is not to be understood as a general and comprehensive moral conception that applies to the political order.'[21] Until now nothing has been said in a positive way about the specific nature of the political. Finally Rawls introduces the third feature of a political conception of justice: 'It is not formulated in terms of a general and comprehensive religious, philosophical or moral doctrine but rather in terms of certain fundamental intuitive ideas viewed as latent in the public political culture of a democratic society.'[22] So we are left with the intuitive ideas to understand in what sense a conception of justice is political. On the other side, as we have seen before, the two main intuitive ideas from which he starts are that society is a fair system of social cooperation and that citizens are free and equal in virtue of their possession of two moral powers – (1) capacity for a sense of justice and (2) capacity for a conception of the good[23] – we are still within the discourse of morality, and his conception of citizenship is hardly a political one.

After presenting his theory of justice as a contribution to moral philosophy, Rawls later declared that it should better be seen as a part of political philosophy.[24] The problem is that since the beginning Rawls has been using a mode of reasoning which is specific to moral discourse and whose effect when applied to the field of politics is to reduce it to a rational process of negotiation among private interests under the constraints of morality. So conflicts, antagonisms, relations of power, forms of subordination and repression simply disappear and we are faced with a typically liberal vision of a plurality of interests that can be regulated without need for a level superior to political decision and where the question of sovereignty is evacuated. As Carl Schmitt pointed out: 'Liberal concepts typically move between ethics and economics. From that polarity they attempt to annihilate the political as a domain of conquering power and repression.'[25] To think politics in terms of moral language, as Rawls does, necessarily leads to neglect of the role played by conflict, power and interest.

Analysing the differences between moral discourse and political discourse from a Wittgensteinian perspective, Hanna Pitkin indicates that, while both concern human action, political discourse alone concerns public action. One of the crucial questions at stake is the creation of a collective identity, a 'we'. In the question 'What shall we do?', the 'we' is not given but rather constitutes a problem. Since in political discourse there is always disagreement about the possible courses of action, the identity of the 'we' that is going to be created through a specific form of collective action might indeed be seen as the central question. For Pitkin, 'Moral discourse is personal dialogue; political discourse concerns a public, a community, and takes place among the members generally. Thus it requires a plurality of viewpoints from which to begin; and the interaction of these varied perspectives, their reconciliation into a single public policy, though that reconciliation will always be temporary, partial and provisional.'[26]

Political discourse attempts to create specific forms of unity among different interests by relating them to a common project and by establishing a frontier to define the forces to be opposed, the 'enemy'. Schmitt is right to assert that 'the phenomenon of the political can be understood only in the context of the ever present possibility of the friend-and-enemy groupings, regardless of the aspects which this possibility implies for morality, aesthetics and economics.'[27] In politics the public interest is always a matter of debate and a final agreement can never be reached; to imagine such a situation is to dream of a society without politics. One should not hope for the elimination of disagreement but for its containment within forms that respect the existence of liberal democratic institutions. As Pitkin argues: 'What characterizes political life is precisely the problem of continually creating unity, a public, in a context of diversity, rival claims and conflicting interests. In the absence of rival claims and conflicting interests, a topic never enters the political realm; no political decision needs to be made. But for the political collectivity, the "we", to act, those continuing claims and interests must be resolved in a way that continues to preserve the collectivity.'[28]

Such a view of the political is completely lacking in Rawls who takes for granted the existence of a common rational self-interest on which the citizens acting as free and equal moral persons can agree and ground principles of justice. He seems to believe that disagreements only concern religious and philosophical questions and that by avoiding those controversial issues it is possible to reach a consensus on the way the basic institutions of society should be organized. He is so confident that there is only one solution to this problem and that rational persons deliberating within the constraints of the reasonable and moved only by their rational advantage will choose his principles of justice, that he considers it would be enough for one man to calculate the rational self-interest of all. In that case the process of deliberation is supererogatory.[29] Politics is not affected by the existence of pluralism, which Rawls understands only as the multiplicity of the conceptions of the good that people exercise in the private sphere, perfectly separated from the public sphere where consensus based on self-interest reigns. This is the perfect liberal utopia. As current controversies about abortion clearly show, pluralism does not mean that all those conflicting conceptions of the good will coexist peacefully without trying to intervene in the public sphere, and the frontier between public and private is not given once and for all but constructed and constantly shifting. Moreover, at any moment 'private' affairs can witness the emergence of antagonisms and thereby become politicized. Therefore Rawls's 'well-ordered society' rests on the elimination of the very idea of the political.

There is another way in which the political is absent in Rawls: the political understood as the symbolic ordering of social relations, the aspect of 'politics in the profound sense, as the ensemble human relations in their real, social structure, in their ability to construct the world'.[30] It is within such an approach, which recalls the classical type of political philosophy and inquires about the different forms of society, the 'regimes' (in the Greek sense of *politeia*), that we can throw light on some problems left unresolved by Rawls. First, what he calls the 'fact of pluralism' is much more than the mere consequence of the acceptance of the principle of toleration; it is the expression of a symbolic mutation – the democratic revolution understood as the end of a hierarchical type of society organized around a single substantive conception of the common good, grounded either in Nature or in God. As Claude Lefort has shown, modern democratic society is constituted 'as a society in which Power, Law and Knowledge are exposed to a radical indeterminacy, a society that has become the theatre of an uncontrollable adventure'.[31] The absence of power embodied in the person of the prince and tied to a transcendental instance pre-empts the existence of a final guarantee or source of legitimation; society can no longer be defined as a substance having an organic identity, and democracy is characterized by the 'dissolution of the markers of certainty'.[32] In a modern democratic society there can no longer be a substantial unity, and division must be recognized as constitutive. Rawls is indeed right in arguing that 'we must abandon the hope of a political community if by such a community we mean a political society united in affirming a general and comprehensive doctrine'.[33] But this is a characteristic feature of the new ordering of social relations and not a consequence to be drawn from the 'fact' of pluralism. If Rawls had possessed such an understanding of the political and been able to see the democratic tradition not as a simple collection of shared meanings, institutions and intuitive ideas but as a specific mode of institution of the social, he would have realized that there could never be, in a modern democracy, a final agreement on a single set of principles of justice.

Secondly, the vague notion of 'intuitive ideas' can be reformulated so as to give equality and freedom a very different status. I agree with Rawls that a theory of justice in a modern democracy should be focused on the means whereby liberty and equality might be realized in our institutions. But the reason is that these are the political principles of the liberal democratic regime. These principles determine a certain type of ordering of the relations that men establish between themselves and their world; they give a specific form to democratic society, shape its institutions, its practices, its political culture; they make possible the constitution of a certain type of individual, create specific forms of political subjectivity and construct particular modes of identity. If equality and liberty are central signifiers for us, it is due to the fact that we have been constructed as subjects in a democratic society whose regime and tradition have put those values at the centre of social life. Without such an understanding of the political as 'disciplinary matrix' of the social (to borrow a term from Thomas Kuhn) it is impossible to go further than the very vague notions of 'shared meanings' and 'intuitive ideas' and the empirical generalizations they imply.

Justice and Hegemony

Liberty and equality constitute the political principles of a liberal democratic regime and should be at the core of a theory of justice in a modern democracy. But there are many possible interpretations of those principles, the type of social relations where they should apply and their mode of institutionalization. Rawls's claim that he has found the rational solution to this question has to be rejected outright. For there cannot be such a solution, providing an undisputed and 'publicly recognized point of view from which all citizens can examine before one another whether or not their political and social institutions are just'.[34] It is the very characteristic of modern democracy to impede such a final fixation of the social order and to preclude the possibility for a discourse to establish a definite suture. Different discourses will, indeed, attempt to dominate the field of discursivity and create nodal points through the practice of articulation, but they can only succeed in temporarily fixing meaning.

Part of the struggle characteristic of modern politics is to constitute a certain order, to fix social relations around nodal points, but successes are necessarily partial and precarious because of the permanence of antagonistic forces. Discourses about justice are part of that struggle because, by proposing competing interpretations of the principles of liberty and equality, they provide grounds of legitimation for different types of demands, create particular forms of identification, and shape political forces. In other words, they play an important role in the establishment of a specific hegemony and in construing the meaning of 'citizenship' at a given moment. A successful hegemony signifies a period of relative stabilization and the creation of a widely shared 'common sense', but such an overlapping consensus is to be distinguished from the Archimedian point of rational agreement for which Rawls is searching. Far from providing the final, rational solution to the problem of justice – which in a modern democracy is bound to remain a permanent, unresolved question – Justice as Fairness is only one among the possible interpretations of the political principles of equality and liberty. To be sure, it is a progressive interpretation, and in the context of the aggressive reassertion of neo-liberalism and its attacks against welfare rights and the widening of the field of equality, Rawls's intentions are commendable. But it must be seen as an intervention in an ongoing debate and cannot pretend to a privileged status with respect to other more or less radical interpretations. The emphasis put on the rational choice procedure might be of rhetorical value – given the current intellectual context – and it might even produce political effects, but it is no guarantee of objectivity.

Rawls has been accused of collapsing justice into equality and of presenting an equalitarian vision far from faithful to the shared meanings dominant in the United States. But that is not the point; the problem is not how well he reflects the actual values of the Americans, since what is really at stake is their transformation. As John Schaar has argued, Rawls proposes 'a basic shift in our operative definition of equality and he wants to move away from our present understanding of equality of opportunity.'[35] He proposes a new articulation that could – if successful – redefine the 'common sense' of liberal democracies and give a new meaning to citizenship. I believe this is an important task and that we need today a political conception of justice that could provide a pole of identification for democratic forces as well as a new language of citizenship to confront the individualistic conceptions based on efficiency or individual liberty of the Hayek or Nozick type.

But if we agree to approach Rawls's theory from that angle the real question that we should ask is how effective would it be in fulfilling such a role? The test for a discourse aiming at the establishment of new forms of articulation is its adequacy in creating a link between recognized principles and hitherto unformulated demands. Only if it manages to construct new subject positions can it have a real purchase on people's political identities. My impression is that, from that point of view, the chances of Justice as Fairness are not very good. It is a theory elaborated in the era of the 'great society' and addresses a type of democratic politics that has been displaced in the following decades. New political subjects have emerged, new forms of identities and communities have been created, and a traditional type of social democratic conception of justice exclusively centred around economic inequalities is unlikely to capture the imagination of the new social movements. A political conception of justice with little space for the new demands manifest in the women's movement, the gay movement, the ecological and anti-nuclear movement and the various anti-institutional movements, while aiming at defending and deepening ideals of liberty and equality present in our democratic culture, will not be in a position to create the overlapping consensus needed for the establishment of a new hegemony. One should also take account of the fact that a new ideological terrain has been defined by the attacks of the right against state intervention and bureaucratization and its deconstruction requires a discursive strategy that can provide new forms of articulation for anti-state resistances. The shortcomings of Rawls on that count are all too evident since his theory of justice implies a great amount of state intervention.

In 'Spheres of Justice', Michael Walzer proposes a pluralist conception of justice that I consider to be better suited to the defence of an egalitarian ideal today and more sensitive to the present political struggles. Walzer criticizes the ideal of 'simple equality' because it would need continual state intervention, and argues that 'equality cannot be the goal of our politics unless we can describe it in a way that protects us against the modern tyranny of politics, against the domination of the party/state.'[36] The solution of complex equality that he puts forward intends to avoid those problems by distinguishing different spheres of justice with their respective distributive principles. He states that the principles of justice should be pluralistic in form and that different goods should be distributed in accordance with different procedures and by different agents. Even if Walzer does not address directly the question posed by the demands of the new movements, his general approach could be useful to deal with those problems because, contrary to Rawls, he provides us with a pluralistic framework which is crucial for the formulation of an adequate theory of justice and conception of citizenship in the present stage of democratic politics.

Political Philosophy without Foundations

Despite its shortcomings, Rawls's theory of justice poses a series of very important questions for political philosophy. His very incapacity to provide a satisfactory answer to those questions is instructive of the limitations of the liberal approach and indicates the way towards a solution. The great merit of Rawls consists in stressing that in modern democratic societies where there is no longer a single substantive common good and where pluralism is central, a political conception of justice cannot be derived from one particular religious, moral or philosophical conception of the good life. We should reject today the idea of a political community unified by an objective moral order for which some communitarians like Sandel are longing.

If the 'priority of the right over the good' meant only that, it would be unobjectionable. The problem is that Rawls cannot accept that such a priority of the right is the consequence of the symbolic ordering of social relations characteristic of the liberal democratic regime and therefore derivative of an idea of the good constituted by the political principles that define it as a political association. I think the reason is twofold. As I have argued, the political properly speaking is absent in Rawls and the very notion of regime as *politeia* is precluded; secondly, his reliance on a liberal individualistic conception of the subject impedes him from thinking of the subject as discursively constructed through the multiplicity of language games in which a social agent participates. The subject in Rawls remains an origin, it exists independently of the social relations in which it is inscribed.

To be sure, he now insists that what he says about the original position only concerns us qua citizens and that it does not imply a fully fledged theory of the self. But the problem is that even the way he addresses our nature qua citizens is inadequate and does not recognize that a certain type of citizenship is the result of given practices, discourses and institutions. For Rawls equality and liberty are properties of human beings qua moral persons. Against Dworkin's interpretation in terms of natural right,[37] he affirms that Justice as Fairness is not a 'right-based' but a 'conception-based' or 'ideal-based' theory since it is based on intuitive ideas that reflect ideals implicit or latent in a public culture of a democratic society.[38] But, as we have seen, those intuitive ideas are never attributed any concrete status, nor are they placed in any relation to the principles of the regime. No explanation is ever given as to why we happen to have those ideas. Rawls seems to reject the idea of 'natural rights' while being unable to accept that it is only qua citizens of a certain type of political community that we have rights; so his whole conception stands in a vacuum.

My guess is that he has been trying to move away from a universalistic, individualistic and natural-right type of liberal discourse but has not yet succeeded in replacing it with a satisfactory alternative because of his incapacity to think of the collective aspect of human existence as constitutive. The individual remains the *terminus a quo* and the *teminus ad quem*, and that prevents him from conceptualizing the political. I think it is in that context that one should understand his conflation of political discourse with moral discourse and his evasion of the central political notions of power, conflict, division, antagonism and sovereignty, as well as the values that can be realized in collective action.

As a result, what Rawls presents as political philosophy is simply a specific type of moral philosophy, a public morality to regulate the basic structure of society. Indeed he asserts that 'the distinction between political conceptions of justice and other moral conceptions is a matter of scope; that is the range of subjects to which a conception applies, and the wider content a wider range requires.'[39] That is exactly where the problem lies, because I believe that the distinction should be one of nature, not merely of scope. A modern political philosophy should articulate political values, the values that can be realized through collective action and through common belonging to a political association. Its subject matter is the ethics of the political, which should be distinguished from morality.

But Rawls's conception precisely precludes such an understanding of political philosophy: there is no room for a notion of the political common good, no place for a really political definition of citizenship, and he can only conceive of citizens as free and equal moral persons engaged in fair terms of social cooperation. Here his communitarian critics who want to revive the ideals of civic republicanism do have a point. Such a tradition could help us to restore some dignity to political participation and go beyond the liberal conception that can only identify citizenship with the possession of rights or moral powers.

There is nevertheless a danger that needs to be avoided; we cannot go back to a premodern conception and sacrifice the individual to the citizen. A modern conception of citizenship should respect pluralism and individual liberty; every attempt to reintroduce a moral community, to go back to a *universitas*, is to be resisted. One task of a modern democratic political philosophy, as I see it, is to provide us with a language to articulate individual liberty with political liberty so as to construe new subject positions and create different citizens' identities. I consider a theory of justice to have an important role to play in such an endeavour because, as Aristotle noted, 'participation in a common understanding of justice makes a polis.'[40] Nevertheless, it should not be forgotten that under modern conditions the most that a theory of justice can aspire to is to cement a hegemony, to establish a frontier, to provide a pole of identification around a certain conception of citizenship, but in a field necessarily criss-crossed by antagonisms where it will be confronted by opposing forces and competing definitions.

Political philosophy in a modern democratic society should not be a search for foundations but the elaboration of a language providing us with metaphoric redescriptions of our social relations. By presenting us with different interpretations of the democratic ideal of liberty and equality, it will not supply metaphysical foundations for the liberal democratic regime (they cannot exist and it does not need any), but it could help us to defend democracy by deepening and extending the range of democratic practices through the creation of new subject positions within a democratic matrix.

Rawls's theory of justice – even if he is not fully aware of it – belongs to such a struggle and despite all its limitations there is a lot in it which is of value for the advance of democracy. His defence of political liberalism should be reformulated within a discourse that would articulate it with some themes of classical political philosophy and with the valorization of politics of the civic republican tradition. To recognize the Aristotelian insight that man is a *zoon politikon* does not commit us necessarily to a teleological and essentialist conception. Several contemporary theoretical currents converge in stressing how participation in a community of language is the *sine qua non* of the construction of human identity and allow us to formulate the social and political nature of man in a non-essentialist way. It should therefore be possible to combine the defence of pluralism and the priority of right characteristic of modern democracy with a revalorization of the political understood as collective participation in a public sphere where interests are confronted, conflicts resolved, divisions exposed, confrontations staged, and in that way – as Machiavelli was the first to recognize – liberty secured.

Notes

1. Richard Rorty, 'Habermas and Lyotard on Postmodernity', in Richard J. Bernstein, ed., *Habermas and Modernity*, Oxford 1985, p. 162.

2. For this distinction see Hans Blumenberg, *The Legitimacy of the Modern Age*, Boston 1983.

3. Richard Rorty, 'Postmodernist Bourgeois Liberalism', *The Journal of Philosophy*, vol. LXXX, no. 10, October 1983, p. 585.

4. Brian Barry, *The Liberal Theory of Justice*, Oxford 1973, p. 166.

5. John Rawls, *A Theory of Justice*, Oxford 1971, p. 11.

6. John Rawls, 'Kantian Constructivism in Moral Theory', *Journal of Philosophy*, vol. 77, no. 9, September 1980, p. 518.

7. Ibid., p. 519.

8. John Rawls, 'The Idea of an Overlapping Consensus', *Oxford Journal of Legal Studies*, vol. 7, no. 1, Spring 1987, p. 12.

9. John Rawls, 'Justice as Fairness: Political not Metaphysical', *Philosophy and Public Affairs*, vol. 14, no. 3, Summer 1985, p. 225.

10. Ibid., p. 235.

11. Rawls, *A Theory of Justice*, p. 303.

12. Ibid., p. 302.

13. Rawls, 'Justice as Fairness', p. 237 n. 20.

14. Charles Taylor, *Philosophy and the Human Sciences*, Philosophical Papers 2, Cambridge 1985, p. 309.

15. Michael Sandel, *Liberalism and the Limits of Justice*, Cambridge 1982, and 'Morality and the Liberal Ideal', *New Republic*, 7 May 1984. For a more detailed critique of Sandel, see my article 'American Liberalism and its Communitarian Critics' in this volume.

16. William A. Glaston, 'Moral Personality and Liberal Theory', *Political Theory*, vol. 10, no. 4, November 1982, p. 506.

17. Ibid., p. 498.

18. Charles Larmore, *Patterns of Moral Complexity*, Cambridge 1987.

19. This distinction is introduced by Rawls in 'Kantian Constructivism in Moral Theory' to specify the two elements of any notion of social cooperation: the Reasonable refers to a conception of the fair terms of social cooperation and articulates an idea of reciprocity and mutuality; the Rational corresponds to the other element and expresses a conception of each participant's rational advantage.

20. Rawls, 'The Idea of an Overlapping Consensus', p. 23.

21. Ibid., p. 3.

22. Ibid., p. 6.

23. Rawls, 'Justice as Fairness', p. 226 ff.

24. Ibid., p. 224 n. 2.

25. Carl Schmitt, *The Concept of the Political*, Rutgers 1976, p. 71.

26. Hanna Fenichel Pitkin, *Wittgenstein and Justice*, Berkeley 1972, p. 216.

27. Schmitt, p. 35.

28. Pitkin, p. 215.

29. Rawls declares: 'To begin with, it is clear that since the differences among the parties are unknown to them, and everyone is equally rational and similarly situated, each is convinced by the same arguments. Therefore, we can view the choice in the original position from the standpoint of one person selected at random' (*A Theory of Justice*, p. 139). As Bernard Manin has pointed out, what Rawls calls deliberation is a simple process of calculation. See B. Manin 'Volonté générale ou délibération?', *Le Débat*, no. 33, January 1985.

30. Roland Barthes, *Mythologies*, Paris 1957, p. 230.

31. Claude Lefort, *The Political Forms of Modern Society*, Oxford 1986, p. 305.

32. Claude Lefort, *Democracy and Political Theory*, Oxford 1988, p. 19.

33. Rawls, 'The Idea of an Overlapping Consensus', p. 10.

34. Rawls, 'Justice as Fairness', p. 229.

35. John Schaar, *Legitimacy in the Modern State*, Transaction Books, 1981, p. 214.

36. Michael Walzer, *Spheres of Justice*, New York 1983, p. 316.

37. Ronald Dworkin, *Taking Rights Seriously*, Harvard 1977, ch. 6.

38. Rawls, 'Justice as Fairness', p. 236.

39. John Rawls, 'The Priority of Right and Idea of the Good', *Philosophy and Public*

Affairs, vol. 17, no. 4, Fall 1988, p. 252.
   40. Aristotle, *Politics*, Book I, ch. II, 1253a15.

4

Democratic Citizenship and the Political Community

The themes of 'citizenship' and 'community' are being discussed in many quarters of the left today. This is no doubt a consequence of the crisis of class politics and indicates the growing awareness of the need for a new form of identification around which to organize the forces struggling for a radicalization of democracy. I believe that the question of political identity is crucial and that the attempt to construct 'citizens'' identities is one of the important tasks of democratic politics. But there are many different visions of citizenship and vital issues are at stake in their contest. The way we define citizenship is intimately linked to the kind of society and political community we want.

How should we understand citizenship when our goal is a radical and plural democracy? Such a project requires the creation of a chain of equivalence among democratic struggles, and therefore the creation of a common political identity among democratic subjects. For the interpellation 'citizens' to be able to fulfil that role, what conditions must it meet?

These are the problems that I will address, and I will argue that the key question is how to conceive of the nature of the political community under modern democratic conditions. I consider that we need to go beyond the conceptions of citizenship of both the liberal and the civic republican tradition while building on their respective strengths.

To situate my reflections in the context of current discussions, I will begin by engaging with the debate between Kantian liberals and the so-called 'communitarians'. In this way I hope to bring to the fore the specificity of my approach both politically and theoretically.

Liberalism versus Civic Republicanism

What is really at stake between John Rawls and his communitarian critics is the issue of citizenship. Two different languages in which to articulate our identity as citizens are confronting each other. Rawls proposes representing the citizen of a constitutional democracy in terms of equal rights expressed by his two principles of justice. He maintains once citizens see themselves as free and equal persons, they should recognize that to pursue their own different conceptions of the good, they need the same primary goods – that is, the same basic rights, liberties and opportunities – as well as the same all-purpose means such as income and wealth and the same social bases of self-respect. This is why they should agree on a political conception of justice that states that 'all social primary goods – liberty and opportunity, income and wealth and the bases of self-respect – are to be distributed equally, unless an unequal distribution of any or all of these goods is to the advantage of the least favored.'[1] According to that liberal view, citizenship is the capacity for each person to form, revise and rationally pursue his/her definition of the good. Citizens are seen as using their rights to promote their self-interest within certain constraints imposed by the exigency to respect the rights of others. The communitarians object that it is an impoverished conception that precludes the notion of the citizen as one for whom it is natural to join with others to pursue common action in view of the common good. Michael Sandel has argued that Rawls's conception of the self is an 'unencumbered' one which leaves no room for a 'constitutive' community, a community that would constitute the very identity of the individuals. It only allows for an 'instrumental' community, a community in which individuals with their previously defined interests and identity enter with a view to furthering those interests.[2]

For the communitarians the alternative to this flawed liberal approach is the revival of the civic republican view of politics that puts a strong emphasis on the notion of a public good, prior to and independent of individual desires and interests. Such a tradition has almost disappeared today because it has been displaced by liberalism, though it has a long history. It received its full expression in the Italian republics at the end of the Middle Ages but its origins go back to Greek and Roman thought. It was reformulated in England in the seventeenth century by James Harrington, John Milton and other republicans. Later it travelled to the New World through the work of the neo-Harringtonians, and recent studies have shown that it played a very important role during the American Revolution.[3]

Although there are serious problems with the liberal conception of citizenship, we must be aware of the shortcomings of the civic republican solution, too. It does provide us with a view of citizenship much richer than the liberal one, and its conception of politics as the realm where we can recognize ourselves as participants in a political community has obvious appeal for the critics of liberal individualism.

Nevertheless there is a real danger of returning to a premodern view of politics, which does not acknowledge the novelty of modern democracy and the crucial contribution of liberalism. The defence of pluralism, the idea of individual liberty, the separation of Church and State, the development of civil society – all are constitutive of modern democratic politics. They require that a distinction be made between the private and the public domains, the realm of morality and the realm of politics. Contrary to what some communitarians propose, a modern democratic political community cannot be organized around a single substantive idea of the common good. The recovery of a strong participatory idea of citizenship should not be made at the cost of sacrificing individual liberty. This is the point where the communitarian critique of liberalism takes a dangerous conservative turn.

The task, I believe, is not that of replacing one tradition with the other but rather of drawing on both and trying to combine their insights in a new conception of citizenship adequate to a project of radical and plural democracy. While liberalism did certainly contribute to the formulation of the idea of a universal citizenship, based on the assertion that all individuals are born free and equal, it also reduced citizenship to a mere legal status, setting out the rights that the individual holds against the state. The way these rights are exercised is irrelevant as long as their holders do not break the law or interfere with the rights of others. Social cooperation aims only to enhance our productive capacities and facilitate the attainment of each person's individual prosperity. Ideas of public-mindedness, civic activity and political participation in a community of equals are alien to most liberal thinkers.

Civic republicanism, on the contrary, emphasizes the value of political participation and attributes a central role to our insertion in a political community. But the problem arises with the exigency of conceiving the political community in a way that is compatible with modern democracy and liberal pluralism. In other words, we are faced with the old dilemma of how to reconcile the liberties of the ancients with the liberties of the moderns. The liberals argue that the two are incompatible and that today ideas about the 'common good' can only have totalitarian implications. According to them, it is impossible to combine democratic institutions with the sense of common purpose that premodern society enjoyed, and the ideals of 'republican virtue' are nostalgic relics which ought to be discarded. Active political participation, they say, is incompatible with the modern idea of liberty. Individual liberty can only be understood in a negative way as absence of coercion.

This argument, powerfully restated by Isaiah Berlin in 'Two

Concepts of Liberty',[4] is generally used to discredit any attempt to resuscitate the civic republican conception of politics. However, it has recently been challenged by Quentin Skinner, who shows that there is no fundamental necessary incompatibility between the classical republican conception of citizenship and modern democracy.[5] He finds in several forms of republican thought, particularly in Machiavelli, a way of conceiving liberty which, though negative – and therefore modern – includes political participation and civic virtue. It is negative because liberty is conceived as the absence of impediments to the realization of our chosen ends. But it also asserts that it is only as citizens of a 'free state', of a community whose members participate actively in the government, that such individual liberty can be guaranteed. To ensure our own liberty and avoid the servitude that would render its exercise impossible, we must cultivate civic virtues and devote ourselves to the common good. The idea of a common good above our private interest is a necessary condition for enjoying individual liberty. Skinner's argument is important because it refutes the liberals' claim that individual liberty and political participation can never be reconciled. This is crucial for a radical democratic project, but the kind of political community adequate for such an articulation between the rights of the individual and the political participation of the citizen then becomes the question to be addressed.

Modern Democracy and Political Community

Another way to approach the debate between Kantian liberals like Rawls and the communitarians is via the question of the priority of the right over the good; this has a direct relevance to the issue of the modern democratic political community.

For Rawls such a priority indicates that individual rights cannot be sacrificed for the sake of the general welfare, as is the case with utilitarianism, and that the principles of justice impose restrictions on what are the permissible conceptions of the good that individuals are allowed to pursue. This is why he insists that the principles of justice must be derived independently of any particular conception of the good, since they need to respect the existence of a plurality of competing conceptions of the good in order to be accepted by all citizens. His aim here is to defend liberal pluralism, which requires not imposing upon individuals any specific conception of well-being or particular plan of life. For liberals those are private questions bearing on individual morality, and they believe that the individual should be able to organize his/her life according to his/her own wishes, without unnecessary interventions. Hence the centrality of the concept of individual rights and the assertion that principles of justice must not privilege a particular conception of the good life.

I consider this an important principle, which needs defending because it is crucial for modern democratic societies. Indeed, modern democracy is precisely characterized by the absence of a substantive common good. This is the meaning of the democratic revolution as analysed by Claude Lefort,[6] who identifies it with the dissolution of landmarks of certainty. According to Lefort, modern democratic society is a society where power has become an empty space and is separated from law and knowledge. In such a society it is no longer possible to provide a final guarantee, a definite legitimation, because power is no longer incorporated in the person of the prince and associated with a transcendental instance. Power, law and knowledge are therefore exposed to a radical indeterminacy: in my terms, a substantive common good becomes impossible. This is also what Rawls indicates when he asserts that 'We must abandon the hope of a political community if by such a community we mean a political society united in affirming a general and comprehensive doctrine.'[7] If the priority of the right over the good were restricted to that, there would not be anything for me to disagree with. But Rawls wants to establish an absolute priority of the right over the good because he does not recognize that it can only exist in a certain type of society with specific institutions and that it is a consequence of the democratic revolution.

To that the communitarians reply, with reason, that such an absolute priority of the right cannot exist and that it is only through our participation in a community which defines the good in a certain way that we can acquire a sense of the right and a conception of justice. Charles Taylor correctly points out that the mistake with the liberal approach is that 'it fails to take account of the degree to which the free individual with his own goals and aspirations whose just rewards it is trying to protect, is himself only possible within a certain kind of civilization; that it took a long development of certain institutions and practices, of the rule of law, of rules of equal respect, of habits of common deliberation, of common association, of cultural development and so on, to produce the modern individual.'[8]

Where the communitarians lose their way is when some of them, such as Sandel, conclude that there can never be a priority of the right over the good, and that we should therefore reject liberal pluralism and return to a type of community organized around shared moral values and a substantive idea of the common good. We can fully agree with Rawls about the priority of justice as the principal virtue of social and political institutions and in defending pluralism and rights, while admitting that those principles are specific to a certain type of political association.

There is, however, another aspect of the communitarian critique of liberalism which we should not abandon but reformulate. The absence of a single substantive common good in modern democratic societies and the separation between the realm of morality and the realm of politics have, no doubt, signified an incontestable gain in individual freedom. But the consequences for politics have been very damaging. All normative concerns have increasingly been relegated to the field of private morality, to the domain of 'values', and politics has been stripped of its ethical components. An instrumentalist conception has become dominant, concerned exclusively with the compromise between already defined interests. On the other hand, liberalism's exclusive concern with individuals and their rights has not provided content and guidance for the exercise of those rights. This has led to the devaluation of civic action, of common concern, which has caused an increasing lack of social cohesion in democratic societies. The communitarians are right to criticize such a situation and I agree with their attempt to revive some aspects of the classical conception of politics. We do need to re-establish the lost connection between ethics and politics, but this cannot be done by sacrificing the gains of the democratic revolution. We should not accept a false dichotomy between individual liberty and rights, or between civic activity and political community. Our choice is not only one between an aggregate of individuals without common public concern and a premodern community organized around a single substantive idea of the common good. To envisage the modern democratic political community outside of this dichotomy is the crucial challenge.

I have already pointed out how Quentin Skinner indicates a possible form of articulation between individual freedom and civic participation. But we must also be able to formulate the ethical character of modern citizenship in a way that is compatible with moral pluralism and respects the priority of the right over the good. What we share and what makes us fellow citizens in a liberal democratic regime is not a substantive idea of the good but a set of political principles specific to such a tradition: the principles of freedom and equality for all. These principles constitute what we can call, following Wittgenstein, a 'grammar' of political conduct. To be a citizen is to recognize the authority of such principles and the rules in which they are embodied, to have them informing our political judgement and our actions. To be associated in terms of the recognition of liberal democratic principles: this is the meaning of citizenship that I want to put forward. It implies seeing citizenship not as a legal status but as a form of identification, a type of political identity: something to be constructed, not empirically given. Since there will always be competing interpretations of the democratic principles of equality and liberty, there will therefore be competing interpretations of democratic citizenship. I will inquire into the nature of a radical democratic citizenship, but before I do, I must return to the question of the political association or community.

The Political Community: Universitas or Societas?

As I indicated previously, we need to conceive of a mode of political association which, although it does not postulate the existence of a substantive common good, nevertheless implies the idea of commonality, of an ethico-political bond that creates a linkage among the participants in the association, allowing us to speak of a political 'community' even if it is not in the strong sense. In other words, what we are looking for is a way to accommodate the distinctions between public and private, morality and politics, that have been the great contribution of liberalism to modern democracy, without renouncing the ethical nature of the political association.

I consider that, if we interpret them in a certain way, the reflections on civil association proposed by Michael Oakeshott in *On Human Conduct* can be very illuminating for such a purpose. Oakeshott shows that *societas* and *universitas*, which were understood in the late Middle Ages as two different modes of human association, can also represent two alternative interpretations of the modern state. *Universitas* indicates an engagement in an enterprise to pursue a common substantive purpose or to promote a common interest. It refers therefore to 'persons associated in a manner such as to constitute them a natural person, a partnership of persons which is itself a Person, or in some important respects like a person'.[9]

Contrary to that model of association of agents engaged in a common enterprise defined by a purpose, *societas* or 'civil association' designates a formal relationship in terms of rules, not a substantive relation in terms of common action. 'The idea *societas* is that of agents who, by choice or circumstance, are related to one another so as to compose an identifiable association of a certain sort. The tie which joins them, and in respect of which each recognizes himself to be *socius*, is not that of an engagement in an enterprise to pursue a common substantive purpose or to promote a common interest, but that of loyalty to one another.'[10] It is not a mode of relation, therefore, in terms of common action but a relation in which participants are related to one another in the acknowledgement of the authority of certain conditions in acting.

Oakeshott insists that the participants in a *societas* or *cives* are not associated for a common enterprise nor with a view to facilitating the attainment of each person's individual prosperity; what links them is the recognition of the authority of the conditions specifying their common or 'public' concern, a 'practice of civility'. This public concern or consideration of *cives* Oakeshott calls *respublica*. It is a practice of civility specifying not performances, but conditions to be subscribed to in choosing performances. These consist in a complex of rules or rule-like prescriptions which do not prescribe satisfactions to be sought or actions to be performed but 'moral considerations specifying conditions to be subscribed to in choosing performances'.[11]

It seems to me that Oakeshott's idea of the civil association as *societas* is adequate to define political association under modern democratic conditions. Indeed it is a mode of human association that recognizes the disappearance of a single substantive idea of the common good and makes room for individual liberty. It is a form of association that can be enjoyed among relative strangers belonging to many purposive associations and whose allegiances to specific communities are not seen as conflicting with their membership of the civil association. This would not be possible if such an association were conceived as *universitas*, as purposive association, because it would not allow for the existence of other genuine purposive associations in which individuals would be free to participate.

To belong to the political community what is required is that we accept a specific language of civil intercourse, the *respublica*. Those rules prescribe norms of conduct to be subscribed to in seeking self-chosen satisfactions and in performing self-chosen actions. The identification with those rules of civil intercourse creates a common political identity among persons otherwise engaged in many different enterprises. This modern form of political community is held together not by a substantive idea of the common good but by a common bond, a public concern. It is therefore a community without a definite shape or a definite identity and in continuous re-enactment. Such a conception is clearly different from the premodern idea of the political community, but it is also different from the liberal idea of the political association. For liberalism also sees political association as a form of purposive association, of enterprise, except that in its case the aim is an instrumental one: the promotion of self-interest.

Oakeshott criticizes the liberal view of the state as a conciliator of interests, which he considers to be as remote from civil association as the idea of the state as promoter of an interest, and he declares 'it has been thought that the "Rule of Law" is enough to identify civil association whereas what is significant is the kind of law: "moral" or "instrumental".'[12] His conception should therefore not be confounded with the liberal doctrine of the Rule of Law. He stresses the moral character of the *respublica* and affirms that political thought concerns the *respublica* in terms of *bonum civile*. He declares: 'Civility, then, denotes an order of moral (not instrumental) considerations, and the so-called neutrality of civil prescriptions is a half truth, which needs to be supplemented by the recognition of civil association as itself a moral and not a prudential condition.'[13] By 'moral' he obviously refers not to a comprehensive view but to what I have proposed calling the 'ethico-political', since he asserts that what is civilly desirable cannot be inferred or derived from general moral principles and that political deliberation is concerned with moral considerations of its own. 'This *respublica* is the articulation of a common concern that the pursuit of all purposes and the promotion of all interests, the satisfaction of all wants and the propagation of all beliefs shall be in subscription to conditions formulated in rules indifferent to the merits of any interest or the truth or error of any belief and consequently not itself a substantive interest or doctrine.'[14]

We could say, using Rawls's vocabulary, that in a civil association or *societas* there exists a priority of the right over the good, but in Oakeshott's case, the principles that specify the right, the *respublica*, are conceived not in a Kantian manner as in Rawls, but in a Hegelian way, since for him, to be associated in terms of the recognition of the *respublica* is to enjoy a *sittlich* relation. What I find useful in this approach is that, while allowing for the recognition of pluralism and individual liberty, the notion of *societas* does not relinquish all normative aspects to the sphere of private morality. This mode of association – which Oakeshott traces back to Machiavelli, Montesquieu and Hegel – permits us to maintain a certain idea of the political community in the sense of a noninstrumental, an ethical, type of bond among *cives*, while severing it from the existence of a substantive common good.

I mentioned at the outset that, to be useful to a radical democratic project, Oakeshott's reflections needed to be interpreted in a certain way. I am, of course, perfectly aware of the conservative use he makes of the distinction between *societas* and *universitas*, but I believe that it is not the only and necessary one.[15] To be sure, Oakeshott's conservatism resides in the content he puts in the *respublica*, and that can obviously be solved by introducing more radical principles, as I will indicate later. But, more fundamentally, it lies in his flawed idea of politics. For his conception of politics as a shared language of civility is only adequate for one aspect of politics: the point of view of the 'we', the friend's side. However, as Carl Schmitt has rightly pointed out, the criterion of the political is the friend/enemy relation. What is completely missing in Oakeshott is division and antagonism, that is, the aspect of the 'enemy'. It is an absence that must be remedied if we want to appropriate his notion of *societas*.

To introduce conflict and antagonism into Oakeshott's model it is necessary to recognize that the *respublica* is the product of a given hegemony, the expression of power relations, and that it can be challenged. Politics is to a great extent about the rules of the *respublica* and its many possible interpretations; it is about the constitution of the political community, not something that takes place inside the political community as some communitarians would have it. Political life concerns collective, public action; it aims at the construction of a 'we' in a context of diversity and conflict. But to construct a 'we' it must be distinguished from the 'them', and that means establishing a frontier, defining an 'enemy'. Therefore, while politics aims at constructing a political community and creating a unity, a fully inclusive political community and a final unity can never be realized since there will permanently be a 'constitutive outside', an exterior to the community that makes its existence possible. Antagonistic forces will never disappear and politics is characterized by conflict and division. Forms of agreement can be reached but they are always partial and provisional since consensus is by necessity based on acts of exclusion. We are indeed very far from the language of civility dear to Oakeshott!

A Radical Democratic Citizenship

What becomes of the idea of citizenship in such a perspective? If we understand citizenship as the political identity that is created through identification with the *respublica*, a new conception of the citizen becomes possible. First, we are now dealing with a type of political identity, a form of identification, no longer simply with a legal status. The citizen is not, as in liberalism, someone who is the passive recipient of specific rights and who enjoys the protection of the law. It is not that those elements become irrelevant but that the definition of the citizen shifts because the emphasis is put on the identification with the *respublica*. It is a common political identity of persons who might be engaged in many different purposive enterprises and with differing conceptions of the good, but who accept submission to the rules prescribed by the *respublica* in seeking their satisfactions and in performing their actions. What binds them together is their common recognition of a set of ethico-political values. In this case, citizenship is not just one identity among others, as in liberalism, or the dominant identity that overrides all others, as in civic republicanism. It is an articulating principle that affects the different subject positions of the social agent (as I will show when I discuss the public/private distinction) while allowing for a plurality of specific allegiances and for the respect of individual liberty.

Since we are dealing with politics, however, there will be competing forms of identification linked to different interpretations of the *respublica*. In a liberal democratic regime we can conceive of the *respublica* as constituted by the political principles of such a regime: equality and liberty for all. If we put such a content in Oakeshott's notion of *respublica* we can assert that the conditions to be subscribed to and taken into account in acting are to be understood as the exigency of treating the others as free and equal persons. This is clearly open to potentially very radical interpretations. For instance, a radical democratic interpretation will emphasize the numerous social relations where relations of domination exist and must be challenged if the principles of liberty and equality are to apply. It should lead to a common recognition among different groups struggling for an extension and radicalization of democracy that they have a common concern and that in choosing their actions they should subscribe to certain rules of conduct; in other words, it should construct a common political identity as radical democratic citizens.

The creation of political identities as radical democratic citizens depends therefore on a collective form of identification among the democratic demands found in a variety of movements: women, workers, black, gay, ecological, as well as in several other 'new social movements'. This is a conception of citizenship which, through a common identification with a radical democratic interpretation of the principles of liberty and equality, aims at constructing a 'we', a chain of equivalence among their demands so as to articulate them through the principle of democratic equivalence. For it is not a matter of establishing a mere alliance between given interests but of actually modifying the very identity of these forces. This is something that many pluralist liberals do not understand because they are blind to power relations. They agree on the need to extend the sphere of rights in order to include groups hitherto excluded, but they see that process as a smooth one of progressive inclusion into citizenship. This is the typical story as told by T. H. Marshall in his celebrated article 'Citizenship and Social Class'. The problem with such an approach is that it ignores the limits imposed on the extension of pluralism by the fact that some existing rights have been constituted on the very exclusion or subordination of the rights of other categories. Those identities must first be deconstructed if several new rights are to be recognized.

To make possible a hegemony of the democratic forces, new identities are therefore required, and I am arguing here in favour of a common political identity as radical democratic citizens. By that I understand a collective identification with a radical democratic interpretation of the principles of the liberal democratic regime: liberty and equality. Such an interpretation presupposes that those principles are understood in a way that takes account of the different social relations and subject positions in which they are relevant: gender, class, race, ethnicity, sexual orientation, and so on.

Such an approach can only be adequately formulated within a problematic that conceives of the social agent not as a unitary subject but as the articulation of an ensemble of subject positions, constructed within specific discourses and always precariously and temporarily sutured at the intersection of those subject positions. Only with a non-essentialist conception of the subject which incorporates the psychoanalytic insight that all identities are forms of identification can we pose the question of political identity in a fruitful way. A non-essentialist perspective is also needed concerning the notions of *respublica*, *societas* and political community. For it is crucial to see them not as empirical referents but as discursive surfaces. Failure to do so would make the type of politics posited here completely incomprehensible.

On this point a radical democratic conception of citizenship connects with the current debates about 'postmodernity' and the critique of rationalism and universalism. The view of citizenship I am proposing rejects the idea of an abstract universalist definition of the public, opposed to a domain of the private seen as the realm of particularity and difference. It considers that, although the modern idea of the citizen was indeed crucial for the democratic revolution, it constitutes today an obstacle to its extension. As feminist theorists have argued, the public realm of modern citizenship has been based on the negation of women's participation.[16] This exclusion was seen as indispensable to postulate the generality and universality of the public sphere. The distinction public/private, central as it was for the assertion of individual liberty, also led to an identification of the private with the domestic and played an important role in the subordination of women.

To the idea that the exercise of citizenship consists in adopting a universal point of view, made equivalent to Reason and reserved to men, I am opposing the idea that it consists in identifying with the ethico-political principles of modern democracy and that there can be as many forms of citizenship as there are interpretations of those principles.

In this view the public/private is not abandoned but reformulated.

Here again Oakeshott can help us to find an alternative to the limitations of liberalism. *Societas* is, according to him, a civil condition in which every enterprise is 'private' while never immune from the 'public' conditions specified in *respublica*. In a *societas* 'every situation is an encounter between "private" and "public", between an action or an utterance to procure an imagined and wished-for substantive satisfaction and the conditions of civility to be subscribed to in performing it; and no situation is the one to the exclusion of the other.'[17] The wants, choices and decisions are private because they are the responsibility of each individual, but the performances are public because they are required to subscribe to the conditions specified in *respublica*. Since the rules of the *respublica* do not enjoin, prohibit or warrant substantive actions or utterances, and do not tell agents what to do, this mode of association respects individual liberty. But the individual's belonging to the political community and identification with its ethico-political principles are manifested by her acceptance of the common concern expressed in the *respublica*. It provides the 'grammar' of the citizen's conduct.

In the case of a radical democratic citizen, such an approach allows us to visualize how a concern with equality and liberty should inform her actions in all areas of social life. No sphere is immune from those concerns, and relations of domination can be challenged everywhere. Nevertheless we are not dealing with a purposive kind of community affirming one single goal for all its members, and the freedom of the individual is preserved.

The distinction between private (individual liberty) and public (*respublica*) is maintained, as is the distinction between individual and citizen, but they do not correspond to discrete separate spheres. We cannot say: here end my duties as a citizen and begins my freedom as an individual. Those two identities exist in a permanent tension that can never be reconciled. But this is precisely the tension between liberty and equality that characterizes modern democracy. It is the very life of such a regime and any attempt to bring about a perfect harmony, to realize a 'true' democracy, can only lead to its destruction. This is why a project of radical and plural democracy recognizes the impossibility of the complete realization of democracy and the final achievement of the political community. Its aim is to use the symbolic resources of the liberal democratic tradition to struggle for the deepening of the democratic revolution, knowing that it is a never-ending process. My thesis here has been that the ideal of citizenship could greatly contribute to such an extension of the principles of liberty and equality. By combining the ideal of rights and pluralism with the ideas of public spiritedness and ethico-political concern, a new modern democratic conception of citizenship could restore dignity to the political and provide the vehicle for the construction of a radical democratic hegemony.

Notes

1. John Rawls, *A Theory of Justice*, Oxford 1971, pp. 302–3.

2. Michael Sandel, *Liberalism and the Limits of Justice*, Cambridge 1982.

3. For a general presentation of the debate, see my article 'American Liberalism and its Communitarian Critics', in this volume.

4. Isaiah Berlin, 'Two Concepts of Liberty', in *Four Essays on Liberty*, Oxford 1969.

5. Quentin Skinner, 'The Idea of Negative Liberty: Philosophical and Historical Perspective', in R. Rorty, J. B. Schneewind and Q. Skinner, eds, *Philosophy in History*, Cambridge 1984.

6. Claude Lefort, *The Political Forms of Modern Society*, Oxford 1986, p. 305ff.

7. John Rawls, 'The Idea of an Overlapping Consensus', *Oxford Journal of Legal Studies*, vol. 7, no. 1, Spring 1987, p. 10.

8. Charles Taylor, *Philosophy and the Human Sciences*, Philosophical Papers 2, Cambridge 1955, p. 200.

9. Michael Oakeshott, *On Human Conduct*, Oxford 1975, p. 203.

10. Ibid., p. 201.

11. Ibid., p. 182.

12. Ibid., p. 318.

13. Ibid., p. 175.

14. Ibid., p. 172.

15. One of Oakeshott's targets is undoubtedly the idea of redistributive justice and the forms of state intervention that such an idea renders legitimate, but I do not believe that the distinction between *universitas* and *societas* necessarily commits us to reject state intervention as being inherently linked to a conception of the state as a purposive common enterprise. One can perfectly justify state intervention on the basis of a certain interpretation of the *respublica*.

16. See, for instance, Carole Pateman, *The Sexual Contract*, Stanford 1988; and Geneviève Fraisse, *Muse de la raison*, Aix-en-Provence 1989.

17. Oakeshott, *On Human Conduct*, p. 183.

Feminism, Citizenship and Radical Democratic Politics

Two topics have recently been the subject of much discussion among Anglo-American feminists: postmodernism and essentialism. Obviously they are related since the so-called 'postmoderns' are also presented as the main critics of essentialism, but it is better to distinguish them since some feminists who are sympathetic to postmodernism have lately come to the defence of essentialism.[1] I consider that, in order to clarify the issues at stake in that debate, it is necessary to recognize that there is no such thing as 'postmodernism' understood as a coherent theoretical approach and that the frequent conflation of post-structuralism and postmodernism can only lead to confusion. Which is not to deny that we have been witnessing through the twentieth century a progressive questioning of the dominant form of rationality and of the premises of the modes of thought characteristic of the Enlightenment. But this critique of universalism, humanism and rationalism has come from many different quarters and is far from being limited to the authors called 'post-structuralists' or 'postmodernists'. All the innovative currents of this century – Heidegger and the post-Heideggerian philosophical hermeneutics of Gadamer, the later Wittgenstein and the philosophy of language inspired by his work, psychoanalysis and the reading of Freud proposed by Lacan, American pragmatism – have, from diverse standpoints, criticized the idea of a universal human nature, of a universal canon of rationality through which that human nature could be known, as well as the traditional conception of truth. Therefore, if the term 'postmodern' indicates such a critique of Enlightenment universalism and rationalism, it must be acknowledged that it refers to the main currents of twentieth-century philosophy, and there is no reason to single out post-structuralism as a special target. On the other hand, if by 'postmodernism' one wants to designate only the very specific form that such a critique takes in authors such as Lyotard and Baudrillard, there is absolutely no justification for putting in that category people like Derrida, Lacan or Foucault as has generally been the case. Too often a critique of a specific thesis of Lyotard or Baudrillard leads to sweeping conclusions about 'the postmoderns', who by then include all the authors loosely connected with post-structuralism. This type of assimilation is quite unhelpful when not clearly disingenuous.

Once the conflation of postmodernism and post-structuralism has been debunked, the question of essentialism appears in a very different light. Indeed it is with regard to the critique of essentialism that a convergence can be established among many different currents of thought, and similarities found in the work of authors as different as Derrida, Wittgenstein, Heidegger, Dewey, Gadamer, Lacan, Foucault, Freud and others. This is very important because it means that such a critique can take many different forms and that if we want to scrutinize its relevance for feminist politics we must engage with all its modalities and implications and not quickly dismiss it on the basis of some of its versions.

My aim in this article will be to show the crucial insights that an anti-essentialist approach can bring to the elaboration of a feminist politics which is also informed by a radical democratic project. I certainly do not believe that essentialism necessarily entails conservative politics and I am ready to accept that it can be formulated in a progressive way. What I want to argue is that essentialism is inescapably deficient when it comes to the construction of a democratic alternative whose objective is the articulation of the struggles linked to different forms of oppression. I consider that it leads to a view of identity that is at odds with a conception of radical and plural democracy and that it does not allow us to construct the new vision of citizenship that is required by such a politics.

The Question of Identity and Feminism

One common practice among critics of essentialism has been the abandonment of the category of the subject as a rational transparent entity able to confer a homogeneous meaning to the total field of her conduct by being the source of her action. For instance, psychoanalysis has shown that, far from being organized around the transparency of an ego, personality is structured on a number of levels which lie outside of the consciousness and rationality of the agents. It has therefore undermined the idea of the unified character of the subject. Freud's central claim is that the human mind is necessarily subject to division between two systems, of which one is not, and cannot be, conscious. Expanding the Freudian insight, Lacan has shown the plurality of registers – the Symbolic, the Real and the Imaginary – that penetrate any identity, and the place of the subject as the place of the lack which, though represented within the structure, is the empty place that at the same time subverts and is the condition of the constitution of any identity. The history of the subject is the history of his/her identifications and there is no concealed identity to be rescued beyond the latter. There is thus a double movement. On the one hand, a movement of decentring which prevents the fixation of a set of positions around a preconstituted point. On the other hand, and as a result of this *essential* non-fixity, the opposite movement: the institution of nodal points, partial fixations which limit the flux of the signified under the signifier. But this dialectics of non-fixity/fixation is possible only because fixity is not pregiven, because no centre of subjectivity precedes the subject's identifications.

In the philosophy of language of the later Wittgenstein, we also find a critique of the rationalist conception of the subject that indicates that the latter cannot be the source of linguistic meanings since it is through participation in different language games that the world is disclosed to us. We encounter the same idea in Gadamer's philosophical hermeneutics in the thesis that there exists a fundamental unity between thought, language and the world, and that it is within language that the horizon of our present is constituted. A similar critique of the centrality of the subject in modern metaphysics and of its unitary character can be found in several forms in the other authors mentioned earlier. However, my purpose here is not to examine those theories in detail but simply to indicate some basic convergences. I am not overlooking the fact that important differences exist among these very diverse thinkers. But from the point of view of the argument I want to make, it is important to grasp the consequences of their common critique of the traditional status of the subject and of its implications for feminism.

It is often said that the deconstruction of essential identities, which is the result of acknowledging the contingency and ambiguity of every identity, renders feminist political action impossible. Many feminists believe that, without seeing women as a coherent identity, we cannot ground the possibility of a feminist political movement in which women could unite as women in order to formulate and pursue specific feminist aims. Contrary to that view, I will argue that, for those feminists committed to a radical democratic politics, the deconstruction of essential identities should be seen as the necessary condition for an adequate understanding of the variety of social relations where the principles of liberty and equality should apply. It is only when we discard the view of the subject as an agent both rational and transparent to itself, and discard as well the supposed unity and homogeneity of the ensemble of its positions, that we are in a position to theorize the multiplicity of relations of subordination. A single individual can be the bearer of this multiplicity and be dominant in one relation while subordinated in another. We can thus conceive the social agent as constituted by an ensemble of 'subject positions' that can never be totally fixed in a closed system of differences, constructed by a diversity of discourses among which there is no necessary relation, but rather a constant movement of overdetermination and displacement. The 'identity' of such a multiple and contradictory subject is therefore always contingent and precarious, temporarily fixed at the intersection of those subject positions and dependent on specific forms of identification. It is therefore impossible to speak of the social agent as if we were dealing with a unified, homogeneous entity. We have rather to approach it as a plurality, dependent on the various subject positions through which it is constituted within various discursive formations; and to recognize that there is no a priori, necessary relation between the discourses that construct its different subject positions. Yet, for the reasons pointed out earlier, this plurality does not involve the *coexistence* of a plurality of subject positions but rather the constant subversion and overdetermination of one by the others, which make possible the generation of 'totalizing effects' within a field characterized by open and indeterminate frontiers.

Such an approach is extremely important for an understanding of feminist as well as other contemporary struggles. Their central characteristic is that an ensemble of subject positions linked through inscription in social relations, hitherto considered as apolitical, have become loci of conflict and antagonism and have led to political mobilization. The proliferation of these new forms of struggle can only be theoretically tackled when one starts with the dialectics and decentring/recentring described earlier.

In *Hegemony and Socialist Strategy*,[2] Ernesto Laclau and I have attempted to draw the consequences of such a theoretical approach for a project of radical and plural democracy. We argued for the need to establish a chain of equivalence among the different democratic struggles so as to create an equivalent articulation between the demands of women, blacks, workers, gays and others. On this point our perspective differs from other non-essentialist views where the aspect of detotalization and decentring prevails and where the dispersion of subject positions is transformed into an effective separation, as is the case with Lyotard and to some extent with

Foucault. For us, the aspect of articulation is crucial. To deny the existence of an a priori, necessary link between subject positions does not mean that there are not constant efforts to establish between them historical, contingent and variable links. This type of link, which establishes between various positions a contingent, unpredetermined relation, is what we designated as 'articulation'. Even though there is no necessary link between different subject positions, in the field of politics there are always discourses that try to provide an articulation from different standpoints. For that reason every subject position is constituted within an essentially unstable discursive structure, since it is submitted to a variety of articulatory practices that constantly subvert and transform it. This is why there is no subject position whose links with others is definitively assured and, therefore, no social identity that would be fully and permanently acquired. This does not mean that we cannot retain notions like 'working class', 'men', 'women', 'blacks' or other signifiers referring to collective subjects. However, once the existence of a common essence has been discarded, their status must be conceived in terms of what Wittgenstein designates 'family resemblances' and their unity must be seen as the result of the partial fixation of identities through the creation of nodal points.

The acceptance by feminists of such an approach has very important consequences for the way we formulate our political struggles. If the category 'woman' does not correspond to any unified and unifying essence, it is no longer necessary to try to unearth it. The central issues become: How is 'woman' constructed as a category within different discourses? How is sexual difference made a pertinent distinction in social relations? And how are relations of subordination constructed through such a distinction? The whole false dilemma of equality-versus-difference is exploded since we no longer have a homogeneous entity 'woman' facing another homogeneous entity 'man', but a multiplicity of social relations in which sexual difference is always constructed in very diverse ways and where the struggle against subordination has to be visualized in specific and differential forms. To ask whether women should become identical to men in order to be recognized as equal, or whether they should assert their difference at the cost of equality, appears meaningless once essential identities are put into question.[3]

Citizenship and Feminist Politics

As a consequence, the very question of what a feminist politics should be, has to be posed in completely different terms. So far, most feminists concerned with the contribution that feminism could make to democratic politics have been looking either for the specific demands that could express women's interests or for the specific feminine values that should become the model for democratic politics. Liberal feminists have been fighting for a wide range of new rights for women to make them equal citizens, but without challenging the dominant liberal model of citizenship and of politics. Their view has been criticized by other feminists who argue that the present conception of the political is a male one and that women's concerns cannot be accommodated within such a framework. Following Carol Gilligan, they oppose a feminist 'ethics of care' to the male and liberal 'ethics of justice'. Against liberal individualist values, they defend a set of values based on the experience of women *as* women, that is, their experience of motherhood and care exercised in the private realm of the family. They denounce liberalism for having constructed modern citizenship as the realm of the public, identified with men, and for having excluded women by relegating them to the private realm. According to this view, feminists should strive for a type of politics that is guided by the specific values of love, care, the recognition of needs and friendship. One of the clearest attempts to offer an alternative to liberal politics grounded in feminine values is to be found in 'Maternal Thinking' and 'Social Feminism' principally represented by Sara Ruddick and Jean Bethke Elshtain.[4] Feminist politics, they argue, should privilege the identity of 'women as mothers' and the private realm of the family. The family is seen as having moral superiority over the public domain of politics because it constitutes our common humanity. For Elshtain 'the family remains the locus of the deepest and most resonant human ties, the most enduring hopes, the most intractable conflicts.'[5] She considers that it is in the family that we should look for a new political morality to replace liberal individualism. In women's experience in the private realm as mothers, she says, a new model for the activity of citizenship is to be found. The maternalists want us to abandon the male liberal politics of the public informed by the abstract point of view of justice and the 'generalized other' and to adopt instead a feminist politics of the private, informed by the virtues of love, intimacy and concern for the 'concrete other' specific to the family.

An excellent critique of such an approach has been provided by Mary Dietz[6] who shows that Elshtain fails to provide a theoretical argument that links maternal thinking and the social practice of mothering to democratic values and democratic politics. Dietz argues that maternal virtues cannot be political because they are connected with and emerge from an activity that is special and distinctive. They are the expression of an unequal relation between mother and child which is also an intimate, exclusive and particular activity. Democratic citizenship, on the contrary, should be collective, inclusive and generalized. Since democracy is a condition in which individuals aim at being equals, the mother–child relationship cannot provide an adequate model of citizenship.

A different feminist critique of liberal citizenship is provided by Carole Pateman.[7] It is more sophisticated, but has features in common with 'Maternal Thinking'. Pateman's tone bears the traces of radical feminism, for the accent is put, not on the mother/child relation, but on the man/woman antagonism. Citizenship is, according to Pateman, a patriarchal category: who a 'citizen' is, what a citizen does, and the arena within which he acts have been constructed in the masculine image. Although women in liberal democracies are now citizens, formal citizenship has been won within a structure of patriarchal power in which women's qualities and tasks are still devalued. Moreover, the call for women's distinctive capacities to be integrated fully into the public world of citizenship faces what she calls the 'Wollstonecraft dilemma': to demand equality is to accept the patriarchal conception of citizenship that implies that women must become like men, while to insist that women's distinctive attributes, capacities and activities be given expression and valued as contributing to citizenship is to demand the impossible because such difference is precisely what patriarchal citizenship excludes.

Pateman sees the solution to this dilemma in the elaboration of a 'sexually differentiated' conception of citizenship that would recognize women *as* women, with their bodies and all that they symbolize. For Pateman this entails giving political significance to the capacity that men lack: to create life, that is, *motherhood*. She declares that this capacity should be granted equal political relevance for defining citizenship as that which is usually considered the ultimate test of citizenship – a man's willingness to fight and to die for his country. She considers that the traditional patriarchal way of posing an alternative, where either the separation or the sameness of the sexes is valorized, needs to be overcome by a new way of posing the question of women. This can be done through a conception of citizenship that recognizes both the specificity of womanhood and the common humanity of men and women. Such a view 'that gives due weight to sexual difference in a context of civil equality, requires the rejection of a unitary (that is, masculine) conception of the individual, abstracted from our embodied existence and from the patriarchal division between the private and the public.'[8] What feminists should aim for is the elaboration of a sexually differentiated conception of individuality and citizenship that would include 'women *as* women in a context of civil equality and active citizenship'.[9]

Pateman provides many very interesting insights into the patriarchal bias of the social contract theorists and the way in which the liberal individual has been constructed according to the male image. I consider that her own solution, however, is unsatisfactory. Despite all her provisos about the historically constructed aspects of sexual difference, her view still postulates the existence of some kind of essence corresponding to women *as* women. Indeed, her proposal for a differentiated citizenship that recognizes the specificity of womanhood rests on the identification of women *as* women with motherhood. There are for her two basic types of individuality that should be expressed in two different forms of citizenship: men *as* men and women *as* women. The problem according to her is that the category of the 'individual', while based on the male model, is presented as the universal form of individuality. Feminists must uncover that false universality by asserting the existence of two sexually differentiated forms of universality; this is the only way to resolve the 'Wollstonecraft dilemma' and to break free from the patriarchal alternatives of 'othering' and 'saming'.

I agree with Pateman that the modern category of the individual has been constructed in a manner that postulates a universalist, homogeneous 'public' that relegates all particularity and difference to the 'private', and that this has very negative consequences for women. I do not believe, however, that the remedy is to replace it by a sexually differentiated, 'bi-gendered' conception of the individual and to bring women's so-called specific tasks into the very definition of citizenship. It seems to me that such a solution remains trapped in the very problematic that Pateman wants to challenge. She affirms that the separation between public and private is the founding moment of modern patriarchalism because 'the separation of private and public is the separation of the world of natural subjection, i.e. women, from the world of conventional relations and individuals, i.e. men. The feminine, private world of nature, particularity, differentiation, inequality, emotion, love and ties of blood is set apart from the public, universal – and masculine – realm of convention, civil equality and freedom, reason, consent and contract.'[10] It is for that reason that childbirth and motherhood have been presented as the antithesis of citizenship and that they have become the symbol of everything natural that cannot be part of the 'public' but must remain in a separate sphere. By asserting the political value of motherhood, Pateman intends to overcome that distinction and contribute to the deconstruction of the patriarchal conception of citizenship and private and public life. As a result of her essentialism, however, she never deconstructs the very opposition of men/women. This is the reason that she ends up, like the maternalists, proposing an inadequate conception of what should be a democratic politics informed by feminism. This is why she can assert that 'the most profound and complex problem for political theory and practice is how the bodies of humankind and feminine and masculine individuality can be fully incorporated into political life.'[11]

My own view is quite different. I want to argue that the limitations of the modern conception of citizenship should be remedied, not by making sexual difference politically relevant to its definition, but by constructing a new conception of citizenship where sexual difference would become effectively irrelevant. This, of course, requires a conception of the social agent of the kind that I defended earlier: as the articulation of an ensemble of subject positions, corresponding to the multiplicity of social relations in which it is inscribed. This multiplicity is constructed within specific discourses which have no necessary relation but only contingent and precarious forms of articulation. There is no reason why sexual difference should be pertinent in all social relations. To be sure, today many different practices, discourses and institutions do construct men and women (differentially) and the masculine/feminine distinction exists as a pertinent one in many fields. But there is no reason why this should remain the case, and we can well imagine sexual difference becoming irrelevant in many social relations where it is currently found. This is indeed the objective of many feminist struggles.

I am not arguing in favour of a total disappearance of sexual difference as a valid distinction; I am not saying either that equality between men and women requires gender-neutral social relations, and it is clear that, in many cases, to treat men and women equally implies treating them differentially. My thesis is that, in the domain of politics, and as far as citizenship is concerned, sexual difference should not be a valid distinction. I am at one with Pateman in criticizing the liberal, male conception of modern citizenship, but I believe that what a project of radical and plural democracy needs is not a sexually differentiated model of citizenship in which the specific tasks of both men and women would be valued equally, but rather a truly different conception of what it is to be a citizen and to act as a member of a democratic political community.

A Radical Democratic Conception of Citizenship

The problems with the liberal conception of citizenship are not limited to those concerning women, and feminists committed to a project of radical and plural democracy should engage with them all. Liberalism has contributed to the formulation of the notion of universal citizenship, based on the assertion that all individuals are born free and equal, but it has also reduced citizenship to a mere legal status, indicating the rights that the individual holds against the state. The way those rights are exercised is irrelevant as long as their holders do not break the law or interfere with the rights of others. Notions of public-spiritedness, civic activity and political participation in a community of equals are alien to most liberal thinkers. Besides, the public realm of modern citizenship was constructed in a universalistic and rationalistic manner that precluded the recognition of division and antagonism and that relegated to the private all particularity and difference. The distinction public/private, central as it was for the assertion of individual liberty, acted therefore as a powerful principle of exclusion. Indeed, through the identification between the private and the domestic, it played an important role in the subordination of women. Recently, several feminists and other critics of liberalism have been looking to the civic republican tradition for a different, more active conception of citizenship that emphasizes the value of political participation and the notion of a common good, prior and independent of individual desires and interests. Nevertheless, feminists should be aware of the limitations of such an approach and of the potential dangers that a communitarian type of politics presents for the struggle of many oppressed groups. The communitarian insistance on a substantive notion of the common good and shared moral values is incompatible with the pluralism that is constitutive of modern democracy and that I consider to be necessary to deepen the democratic revolution and accommodate the multiplicity of present democratic demands. The problems with the liberal construction of the public/private distinction would not be solved by discarding it, but only by reformulating it in a more adequate way. Moreover, the centrality of the notion of rights for a modern conception of the citizen should be acknowledged, even though these must be complemented by a more active sense of political participation and of belonging to a political community.[12]

The view of citizenship I want to put forward as the one required by a project of radical and plural democracy is that of a form of political identity that consists of an identification with the political principles of modern pluralist democracy, that is, the assertion of liberty and equality for all. It would be the common political identity of persons who might be engaged in many different enterprises and with differing conceptions of the good, but who are bound by their common identification with a given interpretation of a set of ethico-political values. Citizenship is not just one identity among others, as it is in liberalism, nor is it the dominant identity that overrides all others, as it is in civic republicanism. Instead, it is an articulating principle that affects the different subject positions of the social agent, while allowing for a plurality of specific allegiances and for the respect of individual liberty. In this view, the public/private distinction is not abandoned, but is constructed in a different way. The distinction does not correspond to discrete, separate spheres; every situation is an encounter between 'private' and 'public' because every enterprise is private though never immune from the public conditions prescribed by the principles of citizenship. Wants, choices and decisions are private because they are the responsibility of each individual, but performances are public because they have to subscribe to the conditions specified by a particular understanding of the ethico-political principles of the regime which provide the 'grammar' of the citizen's conduct.[13]

It is important to stress here that if we hold to the view that the exercise of citizenship consists in identifying with the ethico-political principles of modern democracy, we must also recognize that there can be as many forms of citizenship as there are interpretations of those principles, and that a radical democratic interpretation is one among others. A radical democratic interpretation will emphasize the numerous social relations in which situations of domination exist that must be challenged if the principles of liberty and equality are to apply. It indicates the common recognition by the different groups struggling for an extension and radicalization of democracy that they have a common concern. This should lead to the articulation of the democratic demands found in a variety of involvements: women, workers, blacks, gays, ecological, as well as other 'new social movements'. The aim is to construct a 'we' as radical democratic citizens, a collective political identity articulated through the principle of democratic *equivalence*. It must be stressed that such a relation of *equivalence* does not eliminate *difference* – that would be simple identity. It is only in so far as democratic differences are opposed to forces or discourses which negate all of them that these differences can be substituted for each other.

The view that I am proposing here is clearly different from the liberal as well as from the civic republican one. It is not a gendered conception of citizenship, but neither is it a neutral one. It recognizes that every definition of a 'we' implies the delimitation of a 'frontier' and the designation of a 'them'. That definition of a 'we' always takes place, then, in a context of diversity and conflict. Contrary to liberalism, which evacuates the idea of the common good, and civic republican-ism, which reifies it, a radical democratic approach views the common good as a 'vanishing point', something to which we must constantly refer when we are acting as citizens, but that can never be reached. The common good functions, on the one hand, as a 'social imaginary': that is, as that which the very impossibility of achieving full representation gives the role of a horizon which is the condition of possibility of any representation within the space that it delimits. On the other hand, it specifies what I have designated, following Wittgenstein, a 'grammar of conduct' that coincides with an allegiance to the constitutive ethico-political principles of modern democracy: liberty and equality for all. Yet, since those principles are open to many competing interpreta-tions, one has to acknowledge that a fully inclusive political community can never be realized. There will always be a 'constitutive outside', an exterior to the community that is the very condition of its existence. Once it is accepted that there cannot be a 'we' without a 'them' and that all forms of consensus are by necessity based on acts of exclusion, the issue can no longer be the creation of a fully inclusive community where antagonism, division and conflict will have disappeared. Hence, we have to come to terms with the very impossibility of a full realization of democracy.

Such a radical democratic citizenship is obviously at odds with the 'sexually differentiated' view of citizenship of Carole Pateman, but it is also at odds with another feminist attempt to offer an alternative to the liberal view of the citizen: the 'group differentiated' conception put forward by Iris Young.[14] Like Pateman, Young argues that modern citizenship has been constructed on a separation between 'public' and 'private' that presents the public as the realm of homogeneity and universality and relegates difference to the private. But she insists that this exclusion affects not only women but many other groups based on differences of ethnicity, race, age, disabilities, and so on. For Young, the crucial problem is that the public realm of citizenship has been presented as expressing a general will, a point of view that citizens have held in common and that transcended their differences. Young argues in favour of a repoliticization of public life that would not require the creation of a public realm in which citizens leave behind their particular group affiliation and needs in order to discuss a presumed general interest or common good. In its place she proposes the creation of a 'heterogeneous public' that provides mechanisms for the effective representation and recognition of the distinct voices and perspectives of those constituent groups that are oppressed or disadvantaged. In order to make such a project possible, she looks for a conception of normative reason that does not pretend to be impartial and universal and that does not oppose reason to affectivity and desire. She considers that, despite its limitations, Habermas's communicative ethics can contribute a good deal to its formulation.

Whereas I sympathize with Young's attempt to take account of other forms of oppression than the ones suffered by women, I nevertheless find her solution of 'group differentiated citizenship' highly problematic. To begin with, the notion of a group that she identifies with comprehensive identities and ways of life might make sense for groups such as Native Americans, but is completely inadequate as a description for many other groups whose demands she wants to take into account, like women, the elderly, the differently abled, and so on. She has an ultimately essentialist notion of 'group', and this accounts for why, in spite of all her disclaimers, her view is not so different from the interest-group pluralism that she criticizes: there are groups with their interests and identities already given, and politics is not about the construction of new identities but about finding ways to satisfy the demands of the various parts in a manner acceptable to all. In fact, one could say that hers is a kind of Habermasian version of interest-group pluralism, according to which groups are not viewed as fighting for egoistic private interests but for justice, and where the emphasis is put on the need for argumentation and publicity. So politics in her work is still conceived as a process of dealing with already constituted interests and identities; whereas, in the approach that I am defending, the aim of a radical democratic citizenship should be the construction of a common political identity that would create the conditions for the establishment of a new hegemony articulated through new egalitarian social relations, practices and institutions. This cannot be achieved without the transformation of existing subject positions; this is why the model of the rainbow coalition favoured by Young can be seen only as a first stage towards the implementation of a radical democratic politics. It might indeed provide many opportunities for a dialogue among different oppressed groups, but for their demands to be articulated around the principle of democratic equivalence, new identities need to be created. In their present state many of these demands are antithetical to each other, and their convergence can only result from a political process of hegemonic articulation, and not simply of free and undistorted communication.

Feminist Politics and Radical Democracy

As I indicated at the outset, there has been a great deal of concern among feminists about the possibility of grounding a feminist politics once the existence of women *as* women is put into question. It has been argued that to abandon the idea of a feminine subject with a specific identity and definable interests was to pull the rug from under feminism as politics. According to Kate Soper, 'feminism, like any other politics, has always implied a banding together, a movement based on the solidarity and sisterhood of women, who are linked by perhaps very little else than their *sameness* and "common cause" as women. If this sameness itself is challenged on the ground that there is no "presence" of womanhood, nothing that the term "woman" immediately expresses, and nothing instantiated concretely except particular women in particular situations, then the idea of a political community built around women – the central aspiration of the early feminist movement – collapses.'[15]

In my view, Soper here constructs an illegitimate opposition between two extreme alternatives: either there is an already given unity of 'womanhood' on the basis of some a priori belonging or, if this is denied, no forms of unity and feminist politics can exist. The absence of a female essential identity and of a pregiven unity, however, does not preclude the construction of multiple forms of unity and common action. As the result of the construction of nodal points, partial fixations can take place and precarious forms of identification can be established around the category 'women' which provide the basis for a feminist identity and a feminist struggle. We find in Soper a type of misunderstanding of the anti-essentialist position that is frequent in feminist writings and that consists in believing that the critique of an essential identity must necessarily lead to the rejection of any concept of identity whatsoever.[16]

In *Gender Trouble*,[17] Judith Butler asks: 'What new shape of politics emerges when identity as a common ground no longer constrains the discourse of feminist politics?' My answer is that to visualize feminist politics in that way presents a much greater opportunity for a democratic politics that aims at the articulation of the various different struggles against oppression. What emerges is the possibility of a project of radical and plural democracy.

To be adequately formulated, such a project requires the discarding of the essentialist idea of an identity of women *as* women as well as the attempt to ground a specific and strictly feminist politics. Feminist politics should be understood not as a separate form of politics designed to pursue the interests of women *as* women, but rather as the pursuit of feminist goals and aims within the context of a wider articulation of demands. Those goals and aims should consist in the transformation of all the discourses, practices and social relations where the category 'woman' is constructed in a way that implies subordination. Feminism, for me, is the struggle for the equality of women. But this should not be understood as a struggle to realize the equality of a definable empirical group with a common essence and identity – that is, women – but rather as a struggle against the multiple forms in which the category 'woman' is constructed in subordination. However, we must be aware of the fact that those feminist goals can be constructed in many different ways, according to the multiplicity of discourses in which they can be framed: Marxist, liberal, conservative, radical separatist, radical democratic, and so on. There are, therefore, by necessity, many feminisms, and any attempt to find the 'true' form of feminist politics should be abandoned. I believe that feminists can contribute to politics a reflection on the conditions for creating an effective equality of women. Such a reflection is bound to be influenced by the existing political and theoretical discourses. Instead of trying to prove that a given form of feminist discourse is the one that corresponds to the 'real' essence of womanhood, one should aim to show how it expands the possibilities for an understanding of women's multiple forms of subordination.

My main argument here has been that, for we feminists committed to a political project whose aim is to struggle against the forms of subordination that exist in many social relations and not only in those linked to gender, an approach that permits us to understand how the subject is constructed through different discourses and subject positions is certainly more adequate than one that reduces our identity to one single position – be it class, race or gender. This type of democratic project is also better served by a perspective that allows us to grasp the diversity of ways in which relations of power are constructed, and helps us to reveal the forms of exclusion present in all pretensions to universalism and in the claims to have found the true essence of rationality. This is why the critique of essentialism and all its different forms – humanism, rationalism, universalism – far from being an obstacle to the formulation of a feminist democratic project, is indeed the very condition of its possibility.

Notes

1. See the issue of the journal *Differences*, vol. 1, no. 2 entitled 'The Essential Difference: Another Look at Essentialism', as well as the recent book by Diana Fuss, *Essentially Speaking*, New York 1989.

2. Ernesto Laclau and Chantal Mouffe, *Hegemony and Socialist Strategy. Towards a Radical Democratic Politics*, London 1985.

3. For an interesting critique of the dilemma of equality-versus-difference, which is inspired by a problematic similar to the one I am defending here, see Joan Scott, *Gender*

and The Politics of History, New York 1988, Part IV. Among feminists the critique of essentialism was first developed by the journal *m/f*, which during its eight years of existence (1978–86) made an invaluable contribution to feminist theory. I consider that this work has not yet been superseded and that the editorials as well as the articles by Parveen Adams still represent the most forceful exposition of the anti-essentialist stance. A selection of the best articles from the twelve issues of *m/f* are reprinted in Parveen Adams and Elisabeth Cowie, eds, *The Woman In Question*, Cambridge, Mass. and London 1990.

4. Sara Ruddick, *Maternal Thinking*, New York 1989; Jean Bethke Elshtain, *Public Man, Private Woman*, Princeton 1981.

5. Jean Bethke Elshtain, 'On "The Family Crisis"', *Democracy*, vol. 3, no. 1, p. 138.

6. Mary G. Dietz, 'Citizenship with a Feminist Face. The Problem with Maternal Thinking', *Political Theory*, vol. 13, no. 1, February 1985.

7. Carole Pateman, *The Sexual Contract*, Stanford 1988, *The Disorder of Women*, Cambridge 1989, as well as numerous unpublished papers on which I will also be drawing, especially the following: 'Removing Obstacles to Democracy: The case of Patriarchy'; 'Feminism and Participatory Democracy: Some Reflections on Sexual Difference and Citizenship'; 'Women's Citizenship: Equality, Difference, Subordination'.

8. Carole Pateman, 'Feminism and Participatory Democracy', unpublished paper presented to the Meeting of the American Philosophical Association, St Louis, Missouri, May 1986, p. 24.

9. Ibid., p. 26.

10. Carole Pateman, 'Feminism and Participatory Democracy', pp. 7–8.

11. Carole Pateman, *The Disorder of Women*, p. 53.

12. I analyse the debate between liberals and communitarians in more detail in my article 'American Liberalism and its Communitarian Critics', in this volume.

13. The conception of citizenship that I am presenting here is developed more fully in my 'Democratic Citizenship and the Political Community', in this volume.

14. Iris Marion Young, 'Impartiality and the Civic Public', in Seyla Benhabib and Drucilla Cornell, eds, *Feminism as Critique*, Minneapolis 1987; 'Polity and Group Difference: A Critique of the Ideal of Universal Citizenship', in *Ethics*, 99, January 1989.

15. Kate Soper, 'Feminism, Humanism and Postmodernism', *Radical Philosophy*, 55, p. 13.

16. We find a similar confusion in Diana Fuss who, as Anna Marie Smith indicates in her review of *Essentially Speaking* (in *Feminist Review*, no. 38, April 1991), does not realize that the repetition of a sign can take place without an essentialist grounding. It is for that reason that she can affirm that constructionism is essentialist as far as it entails the repetition of the same signifiers across different contexts.

17. Judith Butler, *Gender Trouble. Feminism and The Subversion of Identity*, New York 1990, p. xi.

6

Towards a Liberal
Socialism

Can the ideals of socialism survive the collapse of 'actually existing socialism' and overcome the discredit it has brought upon all attempts to struggle against inequality? The very idea of social justice has fallen victim to the anti-collectivist wave, and the project of economic democracy is increasingly presented as a relic of a bygone age dominated by the rhetoric of class struggle.

Recognition of the virtues of pluralist democracy is an important achievement, but it would be a serious setback in the fight for democracy if we were to accept 'actually existing capitalist liberal democracies' as the 'end of history'. There are still numerous social relations where the process of democratization is needed, and the task for the left today is to envisage how this can be done in a way that is compatible with the existence of a liberal democratic regime.

In *Hegemony and Socialist Strategy*[1] we proposed a redefinition of the socialist project in terms of 'radical and plural democracy' and visualized it as the extension of democracy to a wide range of social relations. Our intention was to reinscribe socialist goals within the framework of a pluralist democracy and to insist on the necessity of their articulation with the institutions of political liberalism. If it is necessary to abandon the idea of socialism envisaged as a completely different social system whose realization would require the discarding of the political principles of the liberal democratic regime, this does not mean that we should also abandon the objectives of socialism conceived as one dimension in the struggle for a deepening of democracy. Understood as a process of democratization of the economy, socialism is a necessary component of the project of radical and plural democracy. Consequently, I believe there is an urgent need to advocate a 'liberal socialism' and I want to examine here several works which help us in the task of elaborating such a perspective.

Norberto Bobbio and Italian Liberal Socialism

Norberto Bobbio has long been one of the most eloquent advocates of the need to recognize the value of liberal institutions and the necessity to defend them against the defenders of a 'true democracy'. He has consistently advanced the thesis that socialist goals *could* be realized within the framework of liberal democracy and indeed that they could *only* be realized acceptably within such a framework. For him, far from being a contradiction in terms, liberalism and democracy go necessarily together and for that reason a democratic socialism is bound to be a liberal one. He writes: 'The liberal state is not only the historical but the legal premise of the democratic state. The liberal state and the democratic state are doubly interdependent: if liberalism provides those liberties necessary to the proper exercise of democratic power, democracy guarantees the existence and persistence of fundamental liberties.'[2]

Bobbio belongs to an important tradition of Italian liberal thought that, since the nineteenth century, under the influence of John Stuart Mill, has been receptive to socialist ideas. In the twentieth century it crystallized around the journal *La Rivoluzione Liberale* created by Piero Gobetti, and the movement 'Giustizia e Libertà' founded by Carlo Rosselli, who wrote a book called *Socialismo Liberale* in which he argued that socialism must achieve its goals by the liberal method, within the institutional framework of liberal democracy. The aim of that movement of liberal socialism was to combine socialist objectives with the principles of liberal democracy: constitutionalism, parliamentarism and a competitive multi-party system.[3]

Bobbio follows such an approach when he argues that today such a project requires a new social contract that articulates social justice with civil rights. According to him, the current debate around contractarianism provides the terrain for the democratic left to make an important intervention. He considers that 'The crux of this debate is to see whether, starting with the same incontestable individualistic conception of society and using the same institutional structures, we are able to make a counter-proposal to the theory of social contract which neo-liberals want to put into operation, one which would include in its conditions a principle of distributive justice and which would hence be compatible with the theoretical and practical tradition of socialism.'[4] It is no wonder, then, that Bobbio manifests sympathy for the proposals made by John Rawls in his celebrated book *A Theory of Justice* and that he takes his side against Nozick's defence of the minimal state in *Anarchy, State and Utopia*. Bobbio considers that, as long as democracy is alive and individuals retain a right to determine the terms of a new social contract, they will not be concerned only for the protection of their fundamental rights and property but will also require a clause concerned with distributive justice.

But will such a new social contract provide the solution, as Bobbio believes, to the growing ungovernability of modern industrial societies? Can a social contract that articulates the demands of social justice with individual civil and political rights solve the problems facing complex societies today? Is that the way to escape what he terms the 'paradoxes of democracy'? This is not the point of view of the communitarian critics of liberalism, who assert that, since liberal individualism is the cause of the problems, it cannot be the path to their resolution. In order to answer these questions and assess the adequacy of Bobbio's proposals, we need to examine his diagnosis of democracy and the difficulties that confront it in complex societies.

Bobbio's Conception of Democracy

Bobbio insists, again and again, that we should adopt what he calls a 'minimal definition of democracy' as a form of government 'characterized by a set of rules (primary or basic) which establish *who* is authorized to take collective decisions and *which* procedures are to be applied'.[5] Those 'rules of the game' are designed to facilitate and guarantee the widest participation of the majority of citizens in the decisions which affect the whole of society. The function of some of these rules is to establish what is meant by the general will. They determine who has the right to vote, guarantee that the votes of all the citizens have an equal weight, and specify which type of collective decision is to be put into effect. But in addition to those three rules, there are others which refer to the conditions that must be fulfilled for the exercise in freedom to choose to be a real one. There is, first, the principle of pluralism, according to which a democratic system must guarantee the existence of a plurality of organized political groupings which compete with each other; secondly, voters must be able to choose between alternatives; and finally the minority must be guaranteed the right to become a majority in its turn through the organization of periodical elections.

Bobbio, then, chooses to privilege a procedural or juridico-institutional definition of democracy rather than a substantial, ethical one that stresses the ideal of equality, presented as the objective for which a democratic government should strive. He believes that the most important question for democracy is not 'Who rules?' but 'How do they rule?', and that democracy as a form of government, wherein power comes from below instead of being imposed from above. It is for that reason that he defends representative democracy as the only adequate one for our modern complex societies and dismisses the call for direct democracy made by some radical democrats.

To make democracy compatible with liberalism is one of the main concerns of Bobbio, and it certainly explains many of his choices. He declares for instance that 'democracy can be seen as the natural development of liberalism providing that we have in mind not the ideal, egalitarian aspect of democracy, but its character as a political formula in which, as we have seen, it is tantamount to popular sovereignty.'[6] The crucial link, according to him, is located in the articulation between the two sets of rules constitutive of the democratic game. As indicated above, among the six procedural rules that Bobbio presents as necessary for a political system to be called democratic, some refer to the conditions required for the exercise of the right to vote to be a free one between real alternatives. Bobbio declares that only a liberal state can guarantee the basic rights which such a requisite entails: freedom of opinion, of expression, of speech, of assembly, of association, and so on. He says in this respect that these are the rights on which the liberal state has been founded since its inception, giving rise to the doctrine of the *Rechtsstaat*, or juridical state, in the full sense of the term, that is, the state which not only exercises power *sub lege*, but exercises it within the limits derived from the constitutional recognition of the so-called 'inviolable' rights of the individual. Whatever may be the philosophical basis of these rights, they are the necessary precondition for the mainly procedural mechanisms, which characterize a democratic system, to work properly. The constitutional norms which confer these rights are not rules of the game as such: they are preliminary rules which allow the game to take place.[7]

With respect to the present conditions of democracy and its future, Bobbio proposes to distinguish two main aspects: the advances that could be made and the difficulties facing democratic societies today. According to him the difficulties are the following: 'In a nut-shell, these four enemies of democracy – where I am taking democracy to mean the optimum method for making collective decisions – are the large scale of modern life; the increasing bureaucratization of the state apparatus; the growing technicality of the decisions it is necessary to make; and the trend of civil society towards becoming a mass society.'[8]

Seen from the point of view of unfulfilled promises, the shortcomings of democracy today are the survival of invisible power and of oligarchies, the demise of the individual as the protagonist of political life, the renewed vigour of particular interests, the limited scope for democratic participation, and the failure to create educated citizens. But, except for the case of invisible power, where Bobbio sees a trend that contradicts the basic premises of democracy, he considers that the other problems should be viewed as the necessary consequences of adapting abstract principles to reality. Far from seeing direct democracy as a possible solution, he believes that, besides being impossible, it would only make things worse.

What, then, is the remedy proposed by Bobbio? Can something be done to further the process of democratization in modern advanced societies? Ultimately, Bobbio appears moderately optimistic, but he insists that we should be realistic and abandon all hopes of a 'true democracy', a perfectly reconciled society, a perfect consensus. Modern democracy, he insists, must come to terms with pluralism and this implies that some form of dissent is inevitable. Consensus is necessary, but only as far as the rules of the game are concerned. Those rules, when implemented, are the best guarantees against autocracy and heteronomy, which constantly threaten the struggle for the autonomy that he sees as the driving force of democracy.

Once the illusion of direct democracy has been discarded, says Bobbio, we can begin to envisage how the struggle for more democracy can take place. It can only mean the extension of representative democracy to more and more areas of social life. The central factor is not the emergence of a new type of democracy but a process 'in which quite traditional forms of democracy, such as representative democracy, are infiltrating new spaces, spaces occupied until now by hierarchic or bureaucratic organizations'.[9] That is, we should procede from the democratization of the state to the democratization of society; the task is to struggle against autocratic power in all its forms in order to infiltrate the various spaces still occupied by non-democratic centres of power. The democratization of society requires, for Bobbio, tackling all the institutions from family to school, from big business to public administration, that are not run democratically. He declares that 'Nowadays, if an indicator of democratic progress is needed it cannot be provided by the number of people who have the right to vote, but the number of contexts outside politics where the right to vote is exercised. A laconic but effective way of putting it is to say that the criterion for judging the state of democratization achieved in a given country should no longer be to establish "who" votes, but "where" they can vote.'[10]

Pluralism and Individualism

As we have seen, according to Bobbio liberal socialism can offer a solution to the present shortcomings of democracy by providing a new social contract having at its centre a principle of social justice. The aim is to combine social, political and civil rights, putting them on a strong individualistic foundation by appealing to the principle of the individual as the ultimate source of power. The issue of individualism is presented as crucial by Bobbio, who argues that 'Without individualism, there can be no liberalism.'[11] The compatibility of liberalism and democracy lies for him in the fact that both share a common starting point, the individual, and are therefore grounded in an individualistic conception of society. The modern idea of the social contract represents, in his view, a Copernican revolution in the relationship between individual and society because it indicates the end of an organicist and holistic conception of society and the birth of individualism. By putting the particular individual with her interests, needs and rights at the origin of society, the individualistic conception made possible, not only the liberal state but also the modern idea of democracy, whose fundamental principle is that the source of power is the independent individual, with every individual counting equally. Liberal ideas and democratic procedures could therefore be interwoven and their combination lead to liberal democracy where 'Liberalism defends and proclaims individual liberty as against the state, in both the spiritual and the economic sphere; democracy reconciles individual and society by making society the product of a common agreement between individuals.'[12]

I agree with Bobbio about the importance of individualism in the birth of the modern conception of society, but it seems to me that the real question is to ask whether today such an individualistic conception has not become an obstacle to the extension of democratic ideals. Many of the problems Bobbio finds in modern democracies could be attributed to the effects of individualism. For instance, in their critique of the work of John Rawls, many communitarians have argued that it is precisely the individualistic conception of the subject existing with his rights, prior to and independently of his insertion into society, that is at the origin of our problems. Far from seeing the solution in a new social contract, they consider that the very idea of a social contract, with all its atomistic implications, needs to be abandoned. This is why they argue for a revival of the civic republican tradition with its richer conception of citizenship and its view of politics as the realm where we can recognize ourselves as participants in a political community organized around the idea of a shared common good.

It is not my intention to enter into that debate here,[13] but I would like to reflect on some specific problems confronting the extension of democracy today and on the impossibility of resolving them within an individualistic framework. Let me start by indicating my points of convergence with Bobbio. I think he is right to stress the importance of representative democracy and the need to abandon the illusions of direct democracy and perfect consensus existing in a completely transparent society. When he declares that modern democracy must come to terms with pluralism and that, in a modern state, democracy has no alternative but to be pluralistic, I could not agree more. Yet, in my view, it is precisely here that individualism is an obstacle, because it does not allow us to theorize that pluralism in an adequate way. Representative democracy needs to be defended, but we must also acknowledge that its theory is deficient and that we have to formulate new arguments in its favour. As Carl Schmitt has shown convincingly in his critique of parliamentary democracy,[14] the classical theory of parliamentarism has been rendered completely obsolete by the development of the interventionist state. Bobbio does, in fact, seem to agree with such a judgement, since he criticizes the classical conception of representation and recognizes that no constitutional norm has ever been more violated than the veto on binding mandates. He even goes so far as to admit that it could not have been otherwise and declares: Confirmation of the victory – I would dare to say a definitive one – of the representation of interests over impartial political representation is provided by the type of relationship, which is coming to be the norm in most democratic states in Europe, between opposed interests groups (representatives of industrialists and workers respectively) and parliament. This relationship has brought about a new type of social system which is called, rightly or wrongly, 'neo-corporatism'.[15]

Unfortunately Bobbio leaves the question at that point and does not give us a new rationale for representative democracy, one that would take account of the role played by interests groups. His only argument is that direct democracy would do not better but worse. But this is far from satisfactory and does not provide any answer to Schmitt's assertion that 'If in the actual circumstances of parliamentary business, openness and discussion have become an empty and trivial formality, then parliament, as it developed in the nineteenth century, has also lost its previous foundation and its meaning.'[16]

To be sure, Bobbio refers to certain developments within democratic theory that have shifted the emphasis placed by the classical theory of democracy on the idea of 'participation' and 'sovereignty' in order to put the idea of 'control' at the centre of the theory. It could indeed be argued that his insistence on a procedural conception of democracy is proof that he situates himself more in the camp of the realist theorists than the classical ones. The problem is that he often combines elements from the two traditions without realizing they can be in conflict. Can one bring together Schumpeter and Mill in such an unproblematic way as Bobbio seems to believe? And things get even more complicated when it comes to articulating socialism with that already peculiar mixture. Besides insisting on the necessity of a principle of distributive justice and the need to recognize social rights, Bobbio does not really have much to say on the conditions of that articulation.

I submit that, in order to solve the problems facing liberal democracies today and to provide an effective articulation between socialist goals and the principles of liberal democracy, the framework of individualism must be relinquished. I am not postulating a return to an organicist and holistic conception of society which is clearly premodern and hence inadequate for modern democracy. It is simply that I do not accept that the only alternative to such a view is the individualistic conception predominant in liberal theory. It is necessary to theorize the individual, not as a monad, an 'unencumbered' self that exists prior to and independently of society, but rather as a site constituted by an ensemble of 'subject positions', inscribed in a multiplicity of social relations, the member of many communities and participant in a plurality of collective forms of identification. For that reason both the issue of 'representation of interests' and that of 'rights' have to be posed in a wholly different way. The idea of social rights, for instance, needs to be understood in terms of 'collective rights' that are ascribed to specific communities. It is through her inscription in specific social relations, rather than as an individual outside society, that a social agent is granted rights. Some of these rights can, of course, have a universalistic character and apply to all members of the political community, but others will apply only to specific social inscriptions.

What is at stake here is not a rejection of universalism in favour of particularism, but the need for a new type of articulation between the universal and the particular. There is a way in which the abstract universalism of human rights can be used to negate specific identities and to repress some forms of collective identity that apply to specific communities. Without falling back on a view that denies the universal human dimension of the individual and only allows for pure particularism – which is another form of essentialism – it should be possible to conceive of individuality as constituted by the intersection of a multiplicity of identifications and collective identities that constantly subvert each other.

Associational Socialism and Liberal Socialism

Once we have broken from the straitjacket of individualism we can envisage the articulation between liberalism and socialism in a more promising way. In such an endeavour an important source of inspiration is to be found in the current of associational socialism, a third tradition in the history of socialism, which flourished both in France and in Britain during the nineteenth century and continued until the early 1920s. Paul Hirst has recently suggested that the end of the Cold War and certain economic changes in the West have created conditions in which those ideas could become applicable.[17] Using the work of Michael Piore and Charles Sabel, he argues that the current move in several countries toward flexible specialization has increased the importance of regional economic regulation and small- to medium-scale firms. He says that 'Decentralisation and the promotion of economic self-government offer the best prospect of a form of industrial organisation in which the major contributing interests – the providers of capital, management expertise and labour – have an active interest in the continued manufacturing success of the firm.'[18] It is because of that need for democratization and decentralization that, according to him, associational socialism becomes relevant, since its central idea is that economic units should be cooperatively owned self-governing associations.

Like Bobbio, Hirst considers that the objective of socialism must be the deepening of liberal democratic values, and that the realization of its goals should not be seen as requiring a break with constitutional government and the rule of law. He also understands democracy as fundamentally a struggle against all forms of autocratic power, and socialism as a specific dimension of that struggle. He declares: 'If socialism has any relevance today, it is in raising the two linked questions of the democratic governance of private corporations and the democratisation of state administration.'[19] However, unlike Bobbio, he tries to put forward specific proposals to help us visualize what form such a democratization could take.

Hirst sees associational socialism as representing the only challenge to corporate capitalism that respects the principles of liberal democracy. I find his ideas very useful, although – as he himself recognizes – the appropriation of such a tradition must be made in a very selective way given that some of its ideas are now clearly obsolete. Particularly compelling is the argument that associational socialism, because of its emphasis on the plurality and autonomy of enterprises and collective bodies as decision-making agencies, is a means of enhancing the tradition of Western pluralism and liberalism.

Pluralism lies at the very core of modern democracy; if we want a more democratic society, we need to increase that pluralism and make room for a multiplicity of democratically managed forms of associations and communities. Because associational socialism encourages the organization of social life in small units and challenges hierarchy and administrative centralization, Hirst shows how it can provide us with important models for the democratization of corporations and public bodies. 'Education, health, welfare, and community services can be provided by cooperatively or socially owned and democratically managed bodies. Associational socialism permits such bodies to set their own objectives. It is thus compatible with a pluralistic society in which there are distinct sorts of values or organized interests. It can tolerate and, indeed, should welcome, for example, the Catholic Church and the gay community, which provide health and welfare services for their members.'[20]

Obviously pluralism can never be total, since it requires a legal order and a public power. Contrary to the views of certain pluralists criticized by Carl Schmitt – like G. D. Cole and the early Harold Laski – the state can never become merely one association among others; it must have primacy.[21] An associational society needs a state; one important question that therefore needs to be tackled concerns the form that such a pluralist state should take. In Hirst's view, 'A pluralist state defines its *raison d'être* as the assistance and supervision of associations. Its legal task is to ensure equity between associations and to police the conduct of associations. It treats both individuals and associations as real persons, recognizes that individuals can only seek individuality and fulfil themselves through association with others, and accepts that it must protect the rights of both individuals and associations.'[22]

This last point is particularly important and therefore demands further elaboration. In my view it indicates a crucial area of reflection for democratic theory. Associational socialism can give us an insight into ways of overcoming the obstacles to democracy constituted by the two main forms of autocratic power, large corporations and centralized big governments, and show us how to enhance the pluralism of modern societies. It also indicates the necessity of breaking with the universalistic and individualistic modes of thought which have been dominant in the liberal tradition. Today, to think of democracy exclusively in terms of control of power by individuals *uti singuli* is wholly unrealistic. If, as Hirst points out, 'democracy's future at the national level rests less on the choices of individual voters than on the effective representation of organisations representing major social interests',[23] the central issue of democratization becomes: how can antagonistic interests be controlled so that no concentration of interests is allowed to exercise a monopoly on economic or political power and dominate the process of decision-making? Western societies are democratic because of the pluralism of interests that they have been able to secure and the competition that exists among them. Elections in and of themselves do not guarantee democracy if they are only mechanisms for legitimating governments which, once elected, are not responsive to the needs of the citizens. A multiplicity of associations with a real capacity for decision-making and a plurality of centres of power are needed to resist effectively the trends towards autocracy represented by the growth of technocracy and bureaucracy.

It is on this latter point that the tradition of associational socialism can contribute to the deepening of the pluralism that is constitutive of liberal democracy. But this requires a rejection of the atomistic liberal vision of an individual that could exist with her rights and interests prior to and independently of her inscription in a community. While such a vision is often considered to be an intrinsic part of liberalism, it is in fact only the result of the specific type of articulation that was established historically between individualism and political liberalism. To be sure, it is an articulation that has played an important role in the emergence of modern democracy, but it has subsequently become an obstacle to its deepening. Today, an individualistic framework renders impossible the extension of the democratic revolution to an ensemble of social relations whose specificity can only be grasped by recognizing the multiplicity of the identities and subject positions that make up an individual.

It is therefore in its questioning of individualism and in its contribution to the formulation of a new approach to individuality that restores its social nature without reducing it to a simple component of an organic whole, that the socialist tradition of thought can still play an important role. If, as I believe, the elaboration of a non-individualistic conception of the individual is one of our most pressing tasks – in order to enable a new type of relationship between the universal and the particular – it is necessary to free political liberalism from the hindrances of universalism and individualism. And the socialist tradition can provide insights useful for such a task. This is why I think that the articulation between socialism and political liberalism could enrich and deepen the pluralist advances made by liberal democracy and help to institute the framework required for the development of a radical and plural democracy. This is what a liberal socialism sensitive to the multiplicity of democratic struggles should strive for.

Notes

1. Ernesto Laclau and Chantal Mouffe, *Hegemony and Socialist Strategy. Towards a Radical Democratic Politics*, London 1985.

2. Norberto Bobbio, *The Future of Democracy*, Cambridge 1987, p. 25.

3. A good presentation of the historical background of this movement is provided by Perry Anderson in his article 'The Affinities of Norberto Bobbio', now published in *A Zone of Engagement*, London 1992.

4. Ibid., p. 117.

5. Ibid., p. 24.

6. Norberto Bobbio, *Liberalism & Democracy*, London 1990, p. 37.

7. Bobbio, *The Future of Democracy*, p. 25.

8. Norberto Bobbio, *Which Socialism?*, Cambridge 1987, p. 99.

9. Bobbio, *The Future of Democracy*, p. 55.

10. Ibid., p. 56.

11. Bobbio, *Liberalism & Democracy*, p. 9.

12. Ibid., p. 43.

13. I discuss this issue in several articles reprinted in this volume: 'American Liberalism and its Communitarian Critics'; 'Rawls: Political Philosophy without Politics'; and 'Democratic Citizenship and the Political Community'.

14. Carl Schmitt, *The Crisis of Parliamentary Democracy*, trans. E. Kennedy, Cambridge, Mass. and London 1985.

15. Bobbio, *The Future of Democracy*, p. 30.

16. Schmitt, p. 50.

17. Paul Hirst, 'From Statism to Pluralism', in B. Pimlott, A. Wright and T. Flower, eds, *The Alternative*' London 1990.

18. Ibid., p. 21.

19. Paul Hirst, 'Associational Socialism in a Pluralist State', *Journal of Law and Society*, vol. 15, no. 1, Spring 1988, p. 141.

20. Ibid., p. 142.

21. For Schmitt's critique, see Carl Schmitt, *The Concept of the Political*, New Brunswick 1976.

22. Hirst, 'Associational Socialism in a Pluralist State', p. 145.

23. Paul Hirst, 'Representative Democracy and its limits', *The Political Quarterly*, vol. 59, no. 2, April–June 1988, p. 202.

7

On the Articulation between Liberalism and Democracy

In 1964, in an essay entitled 'Post-Liberal-Democracy?', C. B. Macpherson argued that we needed to elaborate a theory of democracy which would sever the links that had been established between the liberal ethical principle of human self-realization and the capitalist market economy. He wrote: 'Fifty years ago the world was almost the preserve of the Western liberal-democratic capitalist societies. Their economies were triumphant, and so were their theories. Since then, two-thirds of the world has rejected the liberal-democratic market society, both in practice and in theory.'[1] Alas, twenty-five years later, the wind seems to be blowing in the opposite direction. From Latin America to Eastern Europe, the market is increasingly presented as a necessary condition for successful democratization, and has become the central symbol of those struggling for the creation of a 'post-communist democracy'.

This does not mean, of course, that Macpherson was mistaken in calling for the development of what he referred to as a 'liberal-democratic socialism.' I think that today such a theory is more needed than ever. At a moment when we are witnessing the beginning of a new political configuration, with left-liberals and post-Marxists entering into a promising dialogue, Macpherson is undoubtedly an important point of reference. His thesis that the ethical values of liberal democracy provide us with the symbolic resources to carry through the struggle for a radical liberal democracy is now being accepted by many forces on the left whose objective is the extension and deepening of the democratic revolution. Indeed, Macpherson's belief in the radical potential of the liberal democratic ideal is shared by those of us who want to redefine socialism in terms of radical and plural democracy.

There are nevertheless some problems with Macpherson's approach, which I intend to raise by contrasting his position with that of a fellow liberal democratic socialist, Norberto Bobbio. Bobbio and Macpherson share a commitment to extending the tradition of liberal democracy in a more radical direction. They want to defend liberal principles while expanding the scope of democratic control, and consider that the crucial question for the left is how to achieve a socialism that is compatible with liberal democracy. There are, however, important differences in the way they visualize such a liberal democratic socialism. Although Bobbio agrees that a greater degree of participation is needed, his model is not one of participatory democracy and he does not put as much emphasis as Macpherson on direct democracy. Nor does Bobbio believe that scarcity could ever be overcome and that we could go beyond the individualistic premisses of liberalism. For him the solution consists in linking those premisses with the notion of distributive justice, as in the Rawlsian type of 'social contract' where social rights provide the basis for the equality required by a modern democratic polity.[2] Macpherson defends the ideals of liberal democracy and its ethical principles, but he is very critical of its institutions. For his part, Bobbio defends those institutions and aims to adapt them to make way for more equality and a greater democratic accountability. At first glance the difference between the two appears to be the classical one between some Eurocommunist form of democratic socialism and social democracy. However, we have increasingly come to recognize that once the reform/revolution dichotomy has been abandoned, such a distinction is not very useful. If commitment to the liberal democratic framework is taken seriously, there can only be different strategies for democratization, to be judged according to their objectives. From that point of view Bobbio often appears more radical than Macpherson, who puts too exclusive an emphasis on economic class relations to the detriment of the demands of the 'new social movements'. For that reason, he does not adequately grasp the extent to which relations of domination have to be challenged to enable the liberal principle of equal rights of self-development to be realized. Bobbio, on the contrary, recognizes that the process of democratization has to extend from the sphere of political relations to encompass all social relations – gender, family, workplace, neighbourhood, school, and so on. The problem for him, therefore, is to combine the democratization of the state with the democratization of society. He states: 'Nowadays, if an indicator of democratic progress is needed it cannot be provided by the number of people who have the right to vote, but the number of contexts outside politics where the right to vote is exercised. A laconic but effective way of putting it is to say that the criterion for judging the state of democratization achieved in a given country should no longer be to establish "who" votes, but "where" they can vote.'[3]

Though I believe Bobbio is right that the process of democratization is not to be conceived exclusively as consisting in the transition from representative democracy to direct democracy, I think he goes astray when he presents representative democracy as the privileged type of democratic institution. For instance, he asserts: 'In short, we can say that the way modern democracy is developing is not to be understood as the emergence of a new type of democracy but rather as a process in which quite traditional forms of democracy, such as representative democracy, are infiltrating new spaces, spaces occupied until now by hierarchic or bureaucratic organizations.'[4] To me this is clearly unsatisfactory. There are many social relations where representative forms of democracy would be completely inadequate, and forms of democracy should therefore be plural and adapted to the type of social relations where democratic principles of liberty and equality will be implemented. Representative democracy is better suited in some cases, direct democracy in others; we should also try to imagine new forms of democracy.

Nevertheless, Bobbio is basically right to call our attention to the fact that we should not expect the emergence of a completely new type of democracy and that liberal institutions are here to stay. In that respect he presents a useful corrective to Macpherson, whose views on the matter are rather ambiguous. Of course, Macpherson does not propose to get rid of liberal political institutions but he often seems to accept them as a *pis aller*, a second best that we have to tolerate due to the weight of tradition and the actual circumstances in Western societies. This is why in 'The Life and Times of Liberal Democracy' he presents his Model 4B of participatory democracy, which combines a pyramidal direct/indirect democratic machinery with a continuing party system, as the most realistic.[5] But he does not disqualify Model 4A, the pyramidal councils system, which, according to him, would be in the best tradition of liberal democracy, despite the fact that the framework of liberal political institutions would have disappeared. This latter is in my view a highly dangerous notion of participatory democracy, which does not take account of the crucial importance for modern democracy of liberal political institutions.

To take seriously the ethical principle of liberalism is to assert that individuals should have the possibility of organizing their lives as they wish, of choosing their own ends, and of realizing them as they think best. In other words, it is to acknowledge that pluralism is constitutive of modern democracy. The idea of a perfect consensus, a harmonious collective will, must therefore be abandoned, and the permanence of conflicts and antagonisms accepted. Once the very possibility of achieving homogeneity is discarded, the necessity of liberal institutions becomes evident. Far from being a mere cover-up for the class divisions of capitalist society, as many participatory democrats seem to believe, such institutions provide the guarantee that individual freedom will be protected against the tyranny of the majority or the domination of the totalitarian party/state. In a modern democracy there no longer exists a substantive idea of the good life on which all rational persons could agree, the pluralism that the fundamental liberal institutions – separation of Church and State, division of powers, the limitation of state power – help to secure. Under modern democratic conditions, characterized by what Claude Lefort calls 'the dissolution of the markers of certainty',[6] the interconnection between liberal institutions and democratic procedures is the necessary condition for the extension of the democratic revolution into new areas of social life. This is why political liberalism is a central component of a project of radical and plural democracy. Bobbio is indeed right to assert that modern democracy must be a pluralistic democracy,[7] and to urge us to acknowledge that socialist goals can only be achieved acceptably within the liberal democratic framework.

I believe that democracy must come to terms with pluralism because under modern conditions, where one can no longer speak of 'the people' as a unified and homogeneous entity with a single general will, the democratic logic of identity of government and governed cannot alone guarantee respect for human rights. It is only by virtue of its articulation with political liberalism that the logic of popular sovereignty can avoid descending into tyranny. We can better understand this danger by examining the critiques of liberal democracy coming from the right, and I want now to show where the rejection of pluralism can lead by discussing Carl Schmitt's challenge to parliamentary democracy.

Carl Schmitt on Parliamentary Democracy

Carl Schmitt is best known for a small number of very provocative theses, one of these being that liberalism negates democracy and democracy negates liberalism. In the preface to the second edition of *The Crisis of Parliamentary Democracy* (1926), he argues that liberalism and democracy need to be distinguished from one another and that, once their respective characteristics are specified, the contradictory nature of modern mass democracy becomes evident. Democracy, declares Schmitt, is the principle that equals are to be treated equally; this necessarily implies that unequals will not be treated equally.

According to him, democracy requires homogeneity, which only exists on the basis of the elimination of heterogeneity. Thus, democracies have always excluded what threatened their homogeneity. He considers that the liberal idea of the equality of all persons as persons is foreign to democracy; it is an individualistic humanitarian ethic and not a possible form of political organization. The idea of a democracy of humankind is, for him, unthinkable because an absolute human equality, an equality without the necessary correlate of inequality, would, he says, be an equality robbed of its value and substance and therefore quite meaningless.[8] The only way we can understand universal and equal suffrage is within a given circle of equals, since it is only when homogeneity exists that equal rights make sense. This is why in the different modern democratic states where universal human equality was established, equal rights has always meant in practice the exclusion of those who did not belong to the state.

Schmitt concludes that modern mass democracy rests on a confusion between the liberal ethic of absolute human equality and the democratic political form of identity of governed and governing. Its crisis results, therefore, from 'the contradiction of a liberal individualism burdened by moral pathos and a democratic sentiment governed essentially by political ideals. A century of historical alliance and common struggle against royal absolutism has obscured the awareness of this contradiction. But the crisis unfolds today ever more strikingly, and no cosmopolitan rhetoric can prevent or eliminate it. It is, in its depths, the inescapable contradiction of liberal individualism and democratic homogeneity.'[9]

This is not the only problem that Schmitt sees with parliamentary democracy. He also criticizes it for being a union between two completely heterogeneous political principles, the one of identity proper to the democratic form of government and the one of representation proper to monarchy. Such a hybrid system is the result of the compromise that the liberal bourgeoisie has managed to establish between absolute monarchy and proletarian democracy by way of combining two opposite principles of government. Schmitt asserts that the representative element constitutes the non-democratic aspect of such a democracy and that as far as parliament provides the representation of political unity, it is in opposition to democracy: 'As democracy, modern mass democracy attempts to realize an identity of governed and governing, and thus it confronts parliament as an inconceivable and outmoded institution. If democratic identity is taken seriously, then in an emergency, no other constitutional institution can withstand the sole criterion of the people's will, however it is expressed.'[10]

Schmitt maintains that the unnatural alliance established in the nineteenth century between liberal parliamentary ideas and democratic ideas has reached its moment of crisis. The parliamentary regime has lost its rationale because the principles on which it justified itself are no longer credible under the circumstances of modern mass democracy. According to him, the essence of liberal parliamentarism is public deliberation of argument and counter-argument, public debate and public discussion. The claim is that through such a process of discussion truth will be reached. This is, he says, a typical rationalist idea that can only be grasped within the context of liberalism understood as a consistent and comprehensive metaphysical system. He argues that 'Normally one only discusses the economic line of reasoning that social harmony and the maximization of wealth follow from the free economic competition of individuals, from freedom of contract, freedom of trade, free enterprise. But all this is only an application of a general liberal principle. It is exactly the same: That the truth can be found through an unrestrained clash of opinions and that competition will provide harmony.'[11]

According to Schmitt, the following has happened. The liberal parliamentary order was based on a series of important divisive issues like religion, morality and economics being confined to the private sphere; this was required in order to create the homogeneity that was the necessary condition for the working of democracy. Parliament could in that way appear as the sphere where individuals, separated from their conflicting interests, could discuss and reach a rational consensus. But with the development of modern mass democracy came the 'total state', which democratic pressures for the extension of rights pushed into intervening in more and more areas of society. The phenomenon of 'depoliticization' characteristic of the previous phase was then reversed and politics began to invade all spheres. Not only did parliament increasingly lose its importance, since many decisions concerning crucial issues started to be taken through different procedures; it also became the arena where antagonistic interests confronted each other. This, for Schmitt, marked the end both of the liberal state and of democracy. He claims that, in such conditions, the view that openness and discussion were the two principles which legitimated parliamentarism has lost all credibility and that parliamentarism has been left without any intellectual foundation: 'There are certainly not many people today who want to renounce the old liberal freedoms, particularly freedom of speech and the press. But on the European continent there are not many more who believe that these freedoms still exist where they could actually endanger the real holders of power. And the smallest number still believe that just laws and the right politics can be achieved through newspaper articles, speeches at demonstrations, and parliamentary debates. But that is the very belief in parliament. If in the actual circumstances of parliamentary business, openness and discussion have become an empty and trivial formality, then parliament, as it developed in the nineteenth century, has also lost its previous foundation and its meaning.'[12]

Schmitt was of course writing those lines in 1923 and his analysis refers particularly to the situation of the Weimar Republic, but it is still relevant today. Current liberal democracies are certainly not on the verge of collapse; however, the enormous literature on the crisis of legitimacy in recent decades, and the growing preoccupation with the massive disaffection from politics, indicate that the problems raised by Schmitt have not yet found a solution.

To be sure, many things have changed in liberal political theory. Any attempt to give an ethical and philosophical justification of parliamentary democracy has been abandoned in favour of what Macpherson has called an 'equilibrium' model of democracy. He shows that such a model does not pretend to have any ethical component and treats citizens simply as political consumers. Its main tenets are: 'First, that democracy is simply a mechanism for choosing and authorizing governments, not a kind of society nor a set of moral ends; and second, that the mechanism consists of a competition between two or more self-chosen sets of politicians (élites) arrayed in political parties, for the votes that will entitle them to rule until the next election.'[13] Many consider today that it is this 'pluralist elitist' conception of democracy that explains the lack of interest and participation in the democratic process, and that we need to recover the ethical appeal that was present in the political theory of liberals like Mill, MacIver or Dewey. This is an important point to which I will return later. For the moment I want only to indicate that if this recovery is to be achieved we must come to terms with Schmitt's critique of parliamentary democracy. Far from having become irrelevant due to subsequent transformations in liberal democracies, such a critique is as pertinent as ever, and in many cases the phenomena he was describing have grown in strength. For instance, many of Bobbio's current preoccupations with the danger of 'invisible power' confirm Schmitt's predictions. Bobbio denounces the reappearance of the *arcana imperi* and the increasing role played by secrecy, in which he sees 'a trend completely at variance with the one that inspired the ideal of democracy as the apotheosis of visible power on the part of the citizens, but on the contrary towards the maximum control of the subjects on the part of those in power'.[14] Evaluations of these phenomena by Bobbio and Schmitt obviously differ, but they both recognize that the problem thus created can undermine the legitimacy of the parliamentary system.

Liberalism and the Political

I think we can learn a great deal from Schmitt's critique of parliamentary democracy without having to follow him in his rejection of liberal democracy. He allows us to become aware of the shortcomings of liberalism that need to be remedied if we want to develop an adequate liberal democratic political philosophy. Reading Schmitt in a critical way can also help us understand the crucial importance of the articulation between liberalism and democracy and the dangers involved in any attempt to renounce liberal pluralism.

Indeed, Schmitt's main target is not democracy but liberalism, whose pluralism he violently opposes. The intellectual core of liberalism resides for him 'in its specific relationship to truth, which becomes a mere function of the eternal competition of opinions'.[15] For Schmitt this is absolutely inadmissible, as is the liberal belief in the openness of opinions and its vision of law as *veritas* and not *auctoritas*. He does not object to democracy per se, which he sees as perfectly compatible with an authoritarian regime. For example, he states that 'Bolshevism and Fascism by contrast are, like all dictatorships, certainly antiliberal but not necessarily antidemocratic.'[16] And he advocates replacing parliamentary democracy with a plebiscitary democracy. This is for him a type of regime nearer to the ideal model of democratic identity, and he asserts that through the democratic plebiscitary procedure of acclamation, it would be possible in a mass democracy to re-establish a more authentic public sphere.[17]

The crucial issue concerns the very nature of modern democracy itself. Schmitt refuses to accept that a new form of society has emerged from the disintegration of the theologico-political model. He does not want to acknowledge that under modern conditions, with the disappearance of a substantive common good and the impossibility of a single homogeneous collective will, democracy cannot be conceived on the ancient model of identity of rulers and ruled. Not only must democracy be of a representative sort, it also requires institutions to guarantee the protection of individual rights. His profound hostility to the effects of the democratic revolution and the fact that, as Claude Lefort has shown, power today 'is linked to the image of an empty place, impossible to occupy, so that those who exercise public authority can never claim to appropriate it',[18] prevent him from seeing any value in liberal political institutions. Such a rejection of liberal pluralism and the political institutions that accompany it can have very dangerous consequences and open the door to totalitarianism. In the case of Schmitt, this needs no demonstration. I am not arguing here that his work prior to his joining the Nazis in 1933 was already tainted by their ideology; it is clear to me that it was not and it is incontestable that Schmitt did his best to impede Hitler's rise to power legally. But his antiliberal conception of democracy also made it possible for him to accept Nazi rule later. I believe that the consequences of rejecting liberal pluralism should be understood by those people on the left who are aiming to achieve a perfect democratic homogeneity and see liberalism only as an obstacle to such an ideal.

We do not have to accept Schmitt's thesis that there is an inescapable contradiction between liberalism and democracy; such a contradiction is only the result of his inability to grasp the specificity of modern democracy, between its two constitutive principals of liberty and equality. They can never be perfectly reconciled, but this is precisely what constitutes for me the principal value of liberal democracy. It is this aspect of nonachievement, incompleteness and openness that makes such a regime particularly suited to modern democratic politics. Unfortunately, this aspect has never been properly theorized, and liberal democracy lacks the political philosophy that could provide it with adequate principles of legitimacy. Schmitt is certainly right to argue that those principles are quite unsatisfactory and in need of reformulation.

Ironically enough, while himself believing that such a reformulation is doomed because of the basic contradiction between liberalism and democracy, Schmitt can be very useful for such a task. His uncompromising critique of liberal rationalism and universalism, with its total lack of understanding of the political, is particularly illuminating and needs to be taken into account if we want to provide liberal democracy with the philosophy it needs.

In *The Concept of the Political* Schmitt argues that the pure and rigorous principle of liberalism cannot give birth to a specifically political conception. Every consistent individualism must negate the political since it requires that the individual remains *terminus a quo* and *terminus ad quem*. In consequence, 'there exists a liberal policy in the form of a polemical antithesis against state, church or other institutions which restrict individual freedom. There exists a liberal policy of trade, church and education, but absolutely no liberal politics, only a liberal critique of politics. The systematic theory of liberalism concerns almost solely the internal struggle against the power of the state.'[19] Liberal individualism is unable to understand the formation of collective identities and it cannot grasp the collective aspect of social life as being constitutive. This is why, according to Schmitt, liberal concepts move between ethics and economics, which can both be conceived in individualistic terms. But liberal thought evades state and politics, it attempts 'to annihilate the political as a domain of conquering power and repression'.[20] For Schmitt, the political is concerned with the relations of friend and enemy, it deals with the creation of a 'we' opposed to a 'them'; it is the realm of 'decision' not free discussion. Its subject matter is conflict and antagonism and these indicate precisely the limits of rational consensus, the fact that every consensus is by necessity based on acts of exclusion.

The liberal idea that the general interest results from the free play of private interests, and that a universal rational consensus could come out of free discussion, blinds liberalism to the phenomenon of the political, which for Schmitt 'can be understood only in the context of the ever present possibility of the friend and enemy grouping, regardless of the aspects which this possibility implies for morality, aesthetics and economics'.[21] Liberalism believes that by confining the divisive issues to the sphere of the private, agreement on procedural rules should be enough to regulate the plurality of interests in society. But this liberal attempt to annihilate the political is bound to fail. The political can never be domesticated or eradicated since, as Schmitt indicates, it can derive its energy from the most varied human endeavours: '[E]very religious, moral, economic, ethical or other antithesis transforms itself into a political one if it is sufficiently strong to group human beings effectively according to friend and enemy.'[22]

I believe that Schmitt is right to point out the deficiencies of liberal individualism with respect to the political. Many of the problems facing liberal democracies today stem from the fact that politics has been reduced to an instrumental activity, to the selfish pursuit of private interests. The limiting of democracy to a mere set of neutral procedures, the transformation of citizens into political consumers, and the liberal insistence on a supposed 'neutrality' of the state, have emptied politics of all substance. It has been reduced to economics and stripped of all ethical components. This, of course, was in part the result of a positive phenomenon: the separation between Church and State and the distinction between public and private. But if the separation between the private domain of morality and the public domain of politics was a great victory for liberalism, it also led to the relegation of all normative aspects to the domain of individual morality. So a real gain in individual freedom also made it possible for an instrumentalist conception of politics to become dominant later with the progressive disqualification of political philosophy and the growth of political science. There is an increasing awareness among political theorists of the need to revive political philosophy and to re-establish the link between ethics and politics. Unfortunately the various approaches taken are unsatisfactory and I do not think they can provide an adequate political philosophy for modern democracy.

Towards a Radical-Liberal-Democratic Political Philosophy

The present revival of political philosophy is dominated by the debate between Kantian liberals and their communitarian critics. In a sense, both aim at recovering the normative aspect of politics which had been cast aside by the dominance of the instrumentalist model. Deontological liberals like John Rawls and Ronald Dworkin want to infuse politics with morality. Following the model set by Kant in *On Perpetual Peace*, they advocate a view of politics bound by norms and guided by morally defined goals. The communitarians, on the other hand, attack liberalism on account of its individualism. They denounce the ahistorical, asocial and disembodied conception of the subject that is implied by the idea of an individual endowed with natural rights pre-existent to society, and reject the thesis of the priority of the right over the good which is at the core of the new liberal paradigm established by Rawls. They want to revive a conception of politics as the realm where we recognize ourselves as participants in a community. Against the Kantian inspiration of 'rights-based' liberals, the communitarians call upon Aristotle and Hegel; against liberalism they appeal to the tradition of civic republicanism. The problem is that some of them, like Michael Sandel and Alasdair MacIntyre, seem to believe that a critique of liberal individualism necessarily implies the rejection of pluralism. So they end up proposing a return to a politics of the common good based on shared moral values.[23] Such a position is clearly incompatible with modern democracy because it leads to a premodern view of the political community as organized around a substantive idea of the common good. I agree that it is important to recover notions of civic virtue, public-spiritedness, common good and political community, which have been discarded by liberalism, but they must be reformulated in a way that makes them compatible with the defence of individual liberty.

However, the solution proposed by the Kantian liberals is not satisfactory either. Independent of the fact that their attempt to provide political liberalism with a new political philosophy questions neither liberal individualism nor its inherent rationalism, what they present as political philosophy is nothing more than a public morality to regulate the basic structure of society. In other words, they do not see any substantive difference between moral philosophy and political philosophy; for them it is only a matter of the field of application. For instance, Rawls asserts that 'the distinction between political conceptions of justice and other moral conceptions is a matter of scope; that is the range of subject to which a conception applies, and the wider content a wider range requires.'[24]

The problem with Rawls is that by failing to distinguish properly between moral discourse and political discourse and by using a mode of reasoning specific to moral discourse, he is unable to recognize the nature of the political. Conflicts, antagonisms, relations of power disappear and the field of politics is reduced to a rational process of negotiation among private interests under the constraints of morality. This is, of course, a typical liberal vision of a plurality of interests that can be regulated without the need for a superior level of political decision-making; the question of sovereignty is evaded. For that reason Rawls believes it is possible to find a rational solution to the question of justice, establishing in that way an undisputed and 'publicly recognized point of view from which all citizens can examine before one another whether or not their political and social institutions are just.'[25]

Against such rationalist denial of the political, it is useful to remember with Carl Schmitt that the defining feature of politics is struggle and that 'There always are concrete human groupings which fight other concrete human groupings in the name of justice, humanity, order, or peace.'[26] Therefore there will always be a debate about the nature of justice and no final agreement can ever be reached. Politics in a modern democracy must accept division and conflict as unavoidable, and the reconciliation of rival claims and conflicting interests can only be partial and provisional. To present, with Rawls and the Kantian liberals, the basis of social unity as consisting in a shared rational conception of justice is certainly more commendable than to see it as a *modus vivendi* secured by a convergence of self- and group-interests. But such an attempt to establish moral limits to the pursuit of private egoism is not going to provide liberal democracy with an adequate political philosophy.

What is at stake is our ability to think the ethics of the political. By that I understand the type of interrogation which is concerned with the normative aspects of politics, the values that can be realized through collective action and through common belonging to a political association. It is a subject matter that should be distinguished from morality, which concerns individual action. Under modern conditions where the individual and the citizen do not coincide because private and public have been separated, a reflection on the autonomous values of the political is required. This is precisely the task of political philosophy, which must be distinguished from moral philosophy.

I consider that such a reflection on the ethics of the political calls for the rediscovery of a notion that was central in classical political philosophy: the notion of 'regime' in the Greek sense of *politeia*, which indicates that all forms of political association have ethical consequences. Therefore the elaboration of a liberal democratic political philosophy should deal with the specific values of the liberal democratic regime, its principles of legitimacy or, to use Montesquieu's term, its 'political principles'. Those are the principles of equality and liberty for all; they constitute the political common good which is distinctive of such a regime. However, there will always be competing interpretations of the principles of liberty and equality, the type of social relations where they should apply, and their mode of institutionalization. The common good can never be actualized, it has to remain a *foyer virtuel* to which we must constantly refer but which cannot have a real existence. It is the very characteristic of modern democracy to impede such a final fixation of the social order and to preclude the possibility of a discourse establishing a definite suture. Different discourses will indeed attempt to dominate the field of discursivity and to create 'nodal points', but they can only succeed in temporarily fixing the meaning of equality and liberty. To put it another way, while politics in a liberal democracy aims at creating a 'we', at constructing a political community, a fully inclusive political community can never be achieved since, as Schmitt tells us, in order to construct a 'we' it must be distinguished from a 'them', and that means establishing a frontier, defining an 'enemy'. There will therefore exist a permanent 'constitutive outside', as Derrida has shown us, an exterior to the community that makes its existence possible. On this point Schmitt's ideas converge with several important trends in contemporary theory which affirm the relational character of every identity, the unavoidable couple identity/difference, and the impossibility of a positivity that would be given without any trace of negativity.[27]

To be useful for the elaboration of a modern political philosophy, the concept of regime must make room for the ideal of division and struggle, for the friend/enemy relation. Schmitt's analysis of the concept of *Verfassung* (constitution) is particularly helpful here, especially when he refers to the 'absolute' concept of the constitution. For him, this indicates the unity of the state understood as the political ordering of social complexity. It presents the social not as an ensemble of relations exterior to the political, something on which neutral political procedural rules are imposed, but as something that can only exist through a specific mode of institution that is provided by the political. Any *Verfassung* always determines a certain configuration of forces, both with respect to the outside by distinguishing one form of political society from another, and with respect to the inside by providing the criteria to distinguish between friend and enemy among the different social forces.[28]

To present Schmitt, as Habermas does, as having a simplistic, one-sided view of politics, is a complete misreading of his work.[29] Schmitt was very much concerned with the role of values in understanding politics and he criticizes liberalism for ignoring this dimension. He rightly stresses the need for common political values in a democracy. Of course Schmitt's solution is unacceptable because he believes in the necessity of a substantive normative and social homogeneity, but he can help us to grasp the complexity of the task before us. The rationalist longing for an undistorted rational communication and for a social unity based on rational consensus is profoundly antipolitical because it ignores the crucial place of passions and affects in politics. Politics cannot be reduced to rationality, precisely because it indicates the *limits* of rationality.

Once we recognize that fact, we can begin thinking about democratic politics and political philosophy in a different way. What we should aim for in a modern democracy is the political creation of a unity through common *identification* with a particular interpretation of its political principles, a specific understanding of citizenship. Political philosophy has an important role to play here, not in deciding the *true* meaning of notions like justice, equality or liberty, but in proposing different *interpretations* of those notions. In that way it will provide diverse and always competing languages in which to construct a range of political identities, different modes of conceiving our role as citizens, and to visualize what kind of political community we want to constitute. Envisaged from the point of view of a 'post-metaphysical' political philosophy, the influence of Macpherson has been decisive. He provided many of us on the left with a language that allowed us to recognize the importance of political liberalism at a time when it was, unlike today, very unfashionable. For that reason, and notwithstanding the critiques that can be addressed to his work, I consider our debt to him to be incontestable, and the project of a radical liberal democracy his legacy.

Notes

1.   Crawford Brough Macpherson, *Democratic Theory: Essays in Retrieval*, Oxford 1973, p. 183.

2. Norberto Bobbio, *The Future of Democracy*, Oxford 1987, pp. 131–37.

3. Ibid., p. 56.

4. Ibid., p. 55.

5. C. B. Macpherson, *The Life and Times of Liberal Democracy*, Oxford 1977, p. 112.

6. Claude Lefort, *Democracy and Political Theory*, Oxford, 1988, p. 19.

7. Bobbio, *The Future of Democracy*, p. 59. I am using the term 'pluralism' here to indicate the end of one substantive conception of the common good to be accepted by all, and not in the way it is used in American political science, as in the 'pluralist-elitist' model.

8. Carl Schmitt, *The Crisis of Parliamentary Democracy*, Cambridge, Mass. 1985, pp. 11–12.

9. Ibid., p. 17.

10. Ibid., p. 15.

11. Ibid., p. 35.

12. Ibid., p. 50.

13. Macpherson, *Life and Times of Liberal Democracy*, p. 78.

14. Bobbio, *Future of Democracy*, p. 97.

15. Schmitt, *Crisis of Parliamentary Democracy*, p. 97.

16. Ibid., p. 35.

17. Ibid., p. 16.

18. Claude Lefort, *The Political Forms of Modern Society*, Oxford 1986, p. 279.

19. Carl Schmitt, *The Concept of the Political*, New Brunswick 1976, p. 70.

20. Ibid., p. 71.

21. Ibid., p. 35.

22. Ibid., p. 37.

23. Michael Sandel, *Liberalism and the Limits of Justice*, Cambridge 1982, and 'Morality and the Liberal Ideal', *New Republic*, 7 May 1984. For a more detailed critique of Sandel, see my article 'American Liberalism and its Communitarian Critics' in this volume.

24. John Rawls, 'The Priority of Right and Ideas of the Good', *Philosophy and Public Affairs*, vol. 17, no. 4, Fall 1988, p. 252.

25. John Rawls, 'Justice as Fairness: Political not Metaphysical', *Philosophy and Public Affairs*, vol. 14, no. 3, Summer 1985, p. 229. This critique of Rawls is developed in my article 'Rawls: Political Philosophy without Politics', in this volume.

26. Schmitt, *Crisis of Parliamentary Democracy*, p. 67.

27. For a development of those theoretical considerations and their consequence for understanding the political, see Ernesto Laclau and Chantal Mouffe, *Hegemony and Socialist Strategy. Towards a Radical Democratic Politics*, London 1985, and Ernesto Laclau, *New Reflections on the Revolution of Our Time*, London 1990.

28. Carl Schmitt, *Verfassungslehre*, Berlin 1980, pp. 204–34.

29. Jürgen Habermas, 'Sovereignty and the Führerdemokratie', *Times Literary Supplement*, 26 September 1986.

8

Pluralism and Modern Democracy: Around Carl Schmitt

Does the downfall of Communism signify the end of history, as Fukuyama proclaims, or the beginning of a new era for the democratic project, now at last freed from the burden of the image of 'actually existing socialism'? We have, in fact, to acknowledge that the victory of liberal democracy is due more to the collapse of its enemy than to its own successes. Far from being in excellent health, there is growing disaffection with political life in the Western democracies and clear signs of a dangerous erosion of democratic values. The rise of the extreme right, the rebirth of fundamentalism, and the creeping marginalization of vast sectors of the population are there to remind us that the situation is far from satisfactory in our own countries.

As Norberto Bobbio points out, the crisis of Communism now presents the affluent democracies with a real challenge. Will they be capable of solving the problems to which that system proved incapable of providing solutions? In his view, it would be very dangerous to imagine that the defeat of Communism has put an end to poverty and the longing for justice. 'Democracy,' he writes, 'has admittedly come out on top in the battle with historical communism. But what resources and ideals does it possess with which to confront those problems that gave rise to the Communist challenge?'[1] I believe it is important to provide an answer to this question and that the moment has come to engage in some uncompromising thinking on the nature of the liberal democratic societies. The disappearance of the spectre of totalitarianism should allow us to approach such an inquiry from a different angle. The point is no longer to provide an apologia for democracy but to analyse its principles, examine its operation, discover its limitations and bring out its potentialities. To do this, we must grasp the specificity of pluralist liberal democracy as a *political* form of society, as a new regime (*politeia*), the nature of which, far from consisting in the articulation of democracy and capitalism, as some claim, is to be sought exclusively on the level of the political.

To establish the parameters for a thoroughgoing study of the liberal democratic regime, its nature and the possibilities it offers, I propose to take as my starting point the work of one of its most brilliant and intransigent opponents, Carl Schmitt. Though Schmitt's criticisms were developed at the beginning of the century, they are, in fact, still pertinent and it would be superficial to believe that the writer's subsequent membership of the National Socialist Party means that we can simply ignore them. On the contrary, I believe it is by facing up to the challenge posed by such a rigorous and perspicacious opponent that we shall succeed in grasping the weak points in the dominant conception of modern democracy, in order that these may be remedied.

Schmitt takes the view that the articulation of liberalism and democracy, which occurred in the nineteenth century, gave birth to a hybrid regime characterized by the union of two absolutely heterogeneous political principles. As he sees it, parliamentary democracy brings about a situation in which the principle of identity proper to the democratic form coexists with the principle of representation specific to monarchy. In *The Crisis of Parliamentary Democracy* he declares that, contrary to the normally accepted view, the principle of parliamentarism, as the pre-eminence of the legislative over the executive, does not belong to the universe of thought of democracy, but to that of liberalism. Unlike many political theorists, Schmitt sees that it was not for reasons of scale – the argument that size would have made the exercise of direct democracy impossible – that representative democracy was instituted. He rightly points out that if it had been for reasons of practical expediency that representatives were entrusted with decision-making on behalf of the people, this could just as easily have been used to justify anti-parliamentary Caesarism.[2] We should not, therefore, in his view, look to the democratic principle of identity for the *ratio* of the parliamentary system, but to liberalism. Hence the importance of grasping the coherence of liberalism as an overall metaphysical system. Schmitt argues that the basic liberal principle around which all the rest revolves is that truth can be arrived at through the unfettered conflict of opinions. For liberalism, there is no final truth, and truth becomes, in that theory, 'a mere function of the eternal competition of opinions'.[3] This, says Schmitt, throws new light on the nature of parliamentarism, the *raison d'être* of which must be sought in its constituting a process of confrontation of opinions, from which the political will is supposed to emerge. Consequently, what is essential in the parliament is 'public deliberation of argument and counter-argument, public debate and public discussions, parley, and all this without taking democracy into account'.[4] It is Schmitt's view that the representative element constitutes the non-democratic aspect of parliamentary democracy in so far as it renders impossible that identity between government and governed inherent in the logic of democracy. There is therefore, as he sees it, a contradiction at the heart of the liberal form of government, which means that liberalism denies democracy and democracy denies liberalism. This becomes clearly visible with the crisis of the parliamentary system we find in modern mass democracy. In that system, public discussion, with its dialectical interplay of opinions, has been replaced by partisan negotiation and the calculation of interests; the parties have become pressure groups, 'calculating their mutual interests and opportunities for power, and they actually agree compromises and coalitions on this basis'.[5]

In Schmitt's view, this came about in the following way. The liberal parliamentary order required that a whole series of disruptive questions concerning morality, religion and the economy be confined to the private sphere. This was a necessary precondition if the parliament was to be able to present itself as the place where individuals, distanced from the conflictual interests which separated them, could discuss and arrive at a rational consensus. In this way, the homogeneity was created which, in Schmitt's view, is required for any democracy to function. The development of modern mass democracy was, however, to lead to the appearance of the 'total state', which would be forced to intervene in an increasing range of fields as a result of democratic pressure for the extension of rights. The phenomenon of 'neutralization' which characterized the previous phase was, then, to give way to an opposite movement of 'politicization' of the various forms of social relations. The consequences of the development of that 'total state' for the parliament were incalculable. Not only did it see its influence diminish, since many decisions, including some of the most important, began to be made in other ways; it also became the arena where antagonistic interests came into conflict. Schmitt's conclusion was that the parliamentary system had lost all credibility since no one could believe any longer in the principles on which is was based. As a result, parliamentary democracy found itself bereft of intellectual foundations. And in 1926, in the preface to the second edition of his critique of parliamentarism, he wrote these words, which should give us pause: 'Even if Bolshevism is suppressed and Fascism held at bay, the crisis of contemporary parliamentarism would not be overcome in the least. For it has not appeared as a result of the appearance of those two opponents; it was there before them and will persist after them. Rather the crisis springs from the consequences of modern mass democracy and, in the last analysis, from the contradiction of a liberal individualism burdened by a moral pathos and a democratic sentiment governed essentially by political ideals... It is, in its depths, the inescapable contradiction of liberal individualism and democratic homogeneity.'[6]

The Nature of Modern Democracy

While not accepting the consequences Schmitt draws, we can nevertheless acknowledge that he has to be taken seriously when he points up the deficiencies of liberal parliamentary democracy. To the extent that its institutions are perceived as mere instrumental techniques, it is improbable that it can be assured of the type of adherence which would guarantee effective participation. The 'political virtue' Montesquieu regarded as indispensable to democracy and which he identified with 'the love of laws and the fatherland' cannot develop in such a context. Now, nothing has occurred since the beginning of the century to remedy this absence of a satisfactory elaboration of what might be called the 'political principles' of representative democracy. On the contrary, it is actually the case that all attempts to provide ethical and philosophical arguments for it have been abandoned. With the development of what C. B. Macpherson has described as the 'equilibrium model', democracy became purely a mechanism for choosing and empowering governments, and has been reduced to a competition between elites. As for the citizens, they are treated as consumers in the political marketplace. Hence there is nothing surprising about the low level of participation in the democratic process found in many Western societies today. How, then, is liberal democracy to be given those 'intellectual foundations' without which it is unable to command solid support? This is the challenge Schmitt's work poses for contemporary political philosophy.

In rising to this challenge, it is important first to grasp the specificity of modern democracy and the central role played by pluralism. By this I mean the recognition of individual freedom, that freedom which John Stuart Mill defends in his essay *On Liberty* as the only freedom worthy of the name, and which he defines as the possibility for every individual to pursue happiness as he sees fit, to set his own goals and attempt to achieve them in his own way. Pluralism is therefore linked to the abandonment of a substantive and unique vision of the common good and of the *eudaemonia* which is constitutive of modernity. It is at the centre of the vision of the world that might be termed 'liberal', and that is why what characterizes modern democracy as a political form of society is the articulation between liberalism and democracy. Unlike many liberals, Schmitt clearly sees that such a regime presupposes that the idea of absolute truth be put in question. Some liberals, on account of their rationalism, in fact imagine that they can retain the idea of a truth that is discoverable by everyone, so long as they are capable of leaving aside their own interests and judging solely from the viewpoint of reason. Now, for Schmitt, in relation to truth, liberalism implies 'renouncing a definite result'.[7] It is precisely for this reason that he denounces the articulation which gave rise to liberal democracy. It is indeed clear in his critique of parliamentary democracy that it is not principally democracy that Schmitt opposes. Democracy, which he defines as a logic of identity between government and governed, between the law and the popular will, is, in his view, perfectly compatible with an authoritarian form of government. Thus he declares that 'Bolshevism and Fascism ... are, like all dictatorships, certainly antiliberal but not necessarily antidemocratic.'[8] Admittedly, many will find such an assertion offensive, but it would be wrong to reject it in the name of the 'true' sense of democracy. What it ought to show us is the extent to which what most of us understand by democracy is determined by its modern, liberal form.

If Schmitt can help us to understand the nature of modern democracy, it is, paradoxically, because he must himself remain blind to it. And there is a very simple reason for this: for him, modernity has never come into being. In *Political Theology* he declares that 'All significant concepts of the modern theory of the State are secularized theological concepts.'[9] What appears as modern politics is merely a secularization of theology, a transformation of theological concepts and attitudes for non-religious ends. There can therefore be no break, nothing new, no previously unknown form of legitimacy can emerge.

The idea that, since the democratic revolution, we are on wholly different ground, in another mode of instituting the social, which demands that we conceive democracy in a modern way, making room for pluralism, is, for Schmitt, strictly unthinkable. There is no possibility, within the scope of this thinking, for liberal democracy as a new and legitimate regime. I believe that the 'unthinkability' this represents for Schmitt is very instructive and that it provides us with a key to the totalitarian phenomenon as consisting in wishing to think democracy in the modern period without liberalism. In my view, it is incorrect to assert, as some do, that Schmitt's thinking was imbued with Nazism before his turnabout of 1933 and his espousal of Hitler's movement. There is, however, no doubt that it was his deep hostility to liberalism which made possible, or which did not prevent, his joining the Nazis.

Reflecting upon the case of Schmitt may thus help us to understand the perils present in certain forms of rejection of liberal democracy, even when those rejections are, like the projects for 'participatory democracy' inspired by the New Left of the sixties, profoundly anti-totalitarian. Such projects often see liberalism merely as a facade behind which the class divisions of capitalist society are concealed. For them, as for Schmitt, parties and the parliamentary system are obstacles to the achievement of a true democratic homogeneity. Similar resonances can be found in the critique levelled at liberalism by the so-called 'communitarian' writers. They too reject pluralism and dream of an organic community.[10] In all these endeavours – which, it should be said, are often well-intentioned and very far from Schmitt's conservative and authoritarian positions – we find the same lack of understanding of modern democracy. In societies where the democratic revolution has taken place and which are, by that token, exposed to what Claude Lefort refers to as 'the dissolution of the markers of certainty',[11] it is necessary to rethink democratic politics in such a way that space is allowed for pluralism and individual freedom. The democratic logic of the identity of government and governed cannot alone guarantee respect for human rights. In conditions where one can no longer speak of the people as if it were a unified and homogenous entity with a single general will, it is only by virtue of its articulation to political liberalism that the logic of popular sovereignty can avoid descending into tyranny.

Liberalism and Politics

If, against Schmitt's view, we restore the legitimacy of the liberal democratic form of government, we may begin to inquire into its political principles. Up to this point, he has helped us – in spite of himself – to grasp the importance of the articulation of the democratic logic of identity and the pluralist logic of liberalism. We now have to examine the liberal problematic in order to determine which of its different elements must be defended and which rejected if the aim is to provide the liberal democratic regime with an ethical and philosophical content. Here again, Schmitt may, by his criticisms, indicate how we should proceed. His challenging of liberal individualism, which, he maintains, is incapable of grasping the nature of the phenomenon of politics is, in my view, most important. In *The Concept of the Political* he writes: 'Liberal thought evades or ignores state and politics and moves instead in a typical always recurring polarity of two heterogenous spheres, namely ethics and economics, intellect and trade, education and property. The critical distrust of state and politics is easily explained by the principles of a system whereby the individual must remain *terminus a quo* and *terminus ad quem.*'[12] Liberal thinking necessarily finds itself blocked on the question of the political, since its individualism prevents it from understanding the formation of collective identities.

Now, for Schmitt, the criterion of the political, its *differentia specifica* is the friend–enemy relation; this involves the creation of a 'we' which stands in opposition to a 'them', and it is located, from the outset, in the realm of collective identifications. The political always has to do with conflicts and antagonisms and cannot but be beyond liberal rationalism since it indicates the limits of any rational consensus and reveals that any consensus is based on acts of exclusion. The liberal belief that the general interest is a product of the free play of private interests, and that a rational universal consensus can be arrived at on the basis of free discussion, must necessarily render liberalism blind to the political phenomenon. In Schmitt's view, that phenomenon can be understood 'only in the context of the ever present possibility of the friend-and-enemy grouping, regardless of the aspects which this possibility implies for morality, aesthetics, and economics'.[13] Liberalism imagines that, by relegating disruptive questions to the private sphere, an agreement on the rules of procedure should be sufficient to administer the plurality of interests that exist in society. However, in Schmitt's view, this attempt to annihilate the political is doomed to failure since the political cannot be domesticated, as it derives its energy from the most diverse sources, and 'every religious, moral, economic, ethical or other antithesis transforms into a political one if it is sufficiently strong to group human beings effectively according to friend and enemy.'[14]

To defend liberalism whilst at the same time accepting the criticisms Schmitt makes of individualism and rationalism, we must separate what constitutes liberal thinking's fundamental contribution to democratic modernity – namely, pluralism and the whole range of institutions characteristic of political liberalism – from the other discourses that are often presented as forming an integral part of liberal doctrine. Here the perspective developed by Hans Blumenberg is particularly helpful.

In his book *The Legitimacy of the Modern Age* Blumenberg discusses the secularization thesis as formulated by Schmitt and Karl Löwith among others.[15] Unlike these writers, he defends the idea that the modern age possesses a truly novel quality in the form of the idea of 'self-assertion'. This emerges as a response to the situation created by scholastic theology's decline into 'theological absolutism', which for him means a set of ideas associated with belief in an omnipotent and completely free God. In his view, in the face of this 'theological absolutism', which made the world seem completely contingent, the only solution was the affirmation of human reason (science, art, philosophy, and so on) as a measure of order and source of value in the world. There is, then, a genuine break, but it coexists with a certain continuity. That continuity is, however, a continuity of problems, not of solutions, and of questions, not of answers. It is around this question that Blumenberg introduces one of his most interesting concepts, that of 'reoccupation': 'What mainly occurred in the process that is interpreted as secularization . . . should be described not as the *transposition* of authentically theological contents into secularized alienation from their origin, but rather as the *reoccupation* of answer positions that had become vacant and whose corresponding questions could not be eliminated.'[16] On this basis, we may then distinguish, as Blumenberg does, between what is truly modern – the idea of self-assertion – and what, like the idea of necessary and inevitable progress, is merely the reoccupation of a medieval position, an attempt to give a modern answer to a premodern question instead of abandoning it, as a rationality conscious of its limits would have done. Rationalism may thus be seen, not as something essential to the idea of human self-assertion, to which the defence of individual liberty and pluralism are linked, but as a hangover from the absolutist medieval problematic. This illusion of providing itself with its own foundations, which accompanied the labour of liberation from theology carried out by the Enlightenment, may therefore be recognized as such without calling into question the other aspect – which is constitutive of modernity – namely, self-assertion. It is when it acknowledges its limitations, and when it completely comes to terms with pluralism and accepts the impossibility of total control and final harmony, that modern reason frees itself from its premodern heritage and the idea of cosmos. This is why, as liberals like Isaiah Berlin have understood, a coherent liberalism cannot but abandon rationalism.

We must, therefore, detach ethical pluralism and political liberalism from the discourse of rationalism in order to reformulate modernity's ideal of 'self-assertion' without recourse to what present themselves as the universal dictates of reason. In this way, it will be possible to detach from the problematic of individualism a crucial notion like that of the individual and re-think it in a wholly other terrain.

The Question of the Neutrality of the State

In order to bring out the ethico-political dimension of the liberal democratic form of government and provide it with principles of legitimacy, the liberal doctrine of the neutrality of the state must be revised. That doctrine of neutrality is linked to a fundamental idea of liberalism, that of 'limited government', and also to the distinction between public and private and the affirmation of pluralism. There are, however, various ways of defending the neutrality thesis and some of these have negative consequences.

Some liberals take the view that, in order fully to respect pluralism and not to interfere with the freedom of individuals to choose their own goals, it is necessary to deny any authority to the state in so far as the possibility of promoting or encouraging a particular conception of the good life is concerned: the state is under an obligation to be absolutely neutral in this sphere. Recently, Charles Larmore even went so far as to declare that 'if liberals are to follow fully the spirit of liberalism, they must also devise a *neutral justification of political neutrality*.'[17] This means that, in advocating liberalism, they should refrain from using arguments such as those advanced by John Stuart Mill or by Kant, which imply the assertion of certain values such as plurality or autonomy.

For the defenders of 'neutrality', any reference to ethical values can only give rise to disagreements, and it is seen as important to avoid the trap of 'perfectionism', that is, the philosophical approach which aims to identify forms of life that are superior and to make these the goal to be realized by political life. They see in this a profoundly antiliberal theory and one that is incompatible with pluralism. Whilst opposing perfectionism, Ronald Dworkin nonetheless attempts to distance himself from the idea of an absolute neutrality. In his view, there is a certain conception of equality at the very heart of liberalism. It is because it must treat all its members as equal that the liberal state must be neutral. Thus he writes: 'Since the citizens of a society differ in their conceptions [of the good life], the government does not treat them as equals if it prefers one conception to another, either because the officials believe that one is intrinsically superior, or because one is held by the more numerous or more powerful groups.'[18] Dworkin takes the view that a justification of the neutrality of the state must not seek to be neutral and that it has to be recognized that liberalism is based on a constitutive morality. As he sees it, 'Liberalism cannot be based on scepticism. Its constitutive morality provides that human beings must be treated as equals by their government, not because there is no right or wrong in political morality, but because that is what is right.'[19] In order to prove this thesis, Dworkin seeks recourse to natural law and the existence of rights 'that are *natural* in the sense that they are not the product of any legislation, or convention, or hypothetical contract.'[20] It is, moreover, in this sense that he interprets the theory of justice of John Rawls, of which he has been a solid advocate since its earliest formulation. In Dworkin's view, 'justice as fairness rests on the assumption of a natural right of all men and women to equality of concern and respect, a right they possess not by virtue of birth or characteristics of merit or excellence but simply as human beings with the capacity to make plans and give justice.'[21] For this reason, he disagrees with the interpretation Rawls has now begun to make of his own theory. Rawls is now, in fact, proposing a more historicist version which emphasizes the place the values specific to our liberal democratic tradition occupy within it; he even asserts that he never had the intention of establishing a theory of justice that would be valid for all societies.[22] Yet this is precisely what Dworkin recommends, believing that a theory of justice must call on 'general . . . principles' and its objective must be to 'try to find some inclusive formula that can be used to measure social justice in any society'.[23]

The problem with a perspective like Dworkin's is that it is a form of liberalism that has not broken with rationalism and that can only think the ethical aspect of the political in terms of an application of the principles of a universalist morality to that field. Under cover of a political philosophy, what he offers us is in fact a 'public morality', that is, something of the order of moral philosophy, which is of little assistance when the task is to elaborate the political principles of the liberal democratic form of government.

What is, in my view, a much more interesting approach to the question of the neutrality of the state is that of Joseph Raz in his book *The Morality of Freedom*. Unlike most liberals, Raz adopts a perfectionist point of view, since he believes the state must take up a position as regards the various possible forms of life: it must promote some forms and forbid others. In his view, the state cannot therefore be neutral and must have the character of an 'ethical state'. The form of perfectionism he defends, however, is not incompatible with liberalism since it also includes pluralism. But the limits of that pluralism are given by what, in his view, constitutes the basic value that must prevail in a liberal and democratic state: personal autonomy or 'self-creation'. The central thesis of his book is that personal freedom, when it is understood as implying a pluralism of values and as having its form of expression in personal autonomy, should be encouraged by political action. Raz is very close to John Stuart Mill, whose 'harm principle' he takes over in a reinterpreted form. For him, this principle refers to the way the state has an obligation to respect certain limits in the promotion of its ideals. In effect, 'given that people should live autonomous lives, the state cannot force them to be moral. All it can do is to provide the conditions of autonomy. Using coercion invades autonomy and thus defeats the purpose of promoting it, unless it is done to promote autonomy by preventing harm.'[24] Autonomy is therefore to serve as a criterion for deciding which institutions and social practices should be fostered by a liberal democratic state.

In spite of my reservations about the appropriateness of subscribing to the cause of perfectionism – even when the 'sting' is taken out of it by pluralism – rather than rejecting the neutrality-versus-perfectionism dichotomy, I consider Raz's approach to be potentially one of the most fruitful in contemporary liberal thought, since it enables us to put the ethical dimension back at the heart of the political and to establish limits for state intervention without postulating the state's neutrality. Another aspect deserving of attention is that the liberalism defended by Raz is one that rejects individualism and defends a conception of the subject close to some communitarian writers, such as Charles Taylor. He thus recognizes that autonomy is not an attribute of individuals independently of their insertion in history, that it is the product of an evolution, and that it requires specific institutions and practices. If this value is central for us, this is because it is constitutive of our liberal democratic tradition. Raz is very far from subscribing to the idea of a political philosophy pursuing objective truth and claiming to establish eternal verities.

Because it combines the fundamental contribution of liberalism – the defence of pluralism and individual freedom – with a conception of the subject which avoids the dangers of individualism, Raz's conception may help us to advance our thinking on the nature of liberal democratic politics. It seems to me, however, that the way in which he conceives pluralism is ultimately unsatisfactory. As in all liberal thinking, what we find here is a pluralism without antagonism. Raz does, admittedly, leave room for competition and he recognizes that not all modes of life are realizable at the same time; but, like Rawls and all the other liberals, he has nothing to contribute on what, for Schmitt, constitutes the criterion of the political, namely the friend–enemy relation. No doubt some will object at this point that the contribution of pluralism is precisely that it enables us to transcend such an opposition, but I believe that to be a dangerous liberal illusion which renders us incapable of grasping the phenomenon of politics. The limits to pluralism are not only empirical limits; they also have to do with the fact that some modes of life and some values are by definition incompatible with others and that it is this very exclusion which constitutes them. We have to take Nietzsche's idea of the 'war of the gods' seriously and accept that, if there is no creation of an 'us' without delimiting a 'them', this relation may at any time become the site of an antagonism and the other may come to be perceived as an enemy. Once we have abandoned the rationalist idea that a formula can be found through which men's different ends might be harmonized, we have to come to terms with the fact that a society from which antagonism has been eliminated is radically impossible. This is why we have to accept with Schmitt that 'the phenomenon of the political can be understood only in the context of the ever present possibility of the friend-and-enemy grouping . . .'[25]

Democracy as Substance or as Procedure?

There is, in contemporary thinking on liberal democracy, another theme connected with that of the neutrality of the state that needs to be rethought. This is the idea that democracy merely consists in a set of procedures. This conception – which is very much in vogue today – is far from new, and even at the beginning of the century Hans Kelsen, the legal philosopher who was Schmitt's most important intellectual opponent, referred to it to justify the parliamentary system. According to Kelsen, it was not the possibility of arriving at truth through discussion that was at the origin of parliamentary democracy, but rather the awareness that there was no possible truth. If liberal democracy has recourse to political parties and parliament as instruments of the general will, it is because it recognizes that a substantial homogeneity can never be achieved. He concludes from this that we have to renounce 'ideal' democracy in favour of 'real' democracy and that a realist vision of politics must conceive modern democracy as being defined by a certain number of procedures among which parliament and parties play a central role.[26]

To Schmitt's vision of democracy as substance, Kelsen therefore opposes a view of democracy that stresses its procedural character and puts the emphasis on its functioning. Whereas Schmitt conceives true democracy as being based on homogeneity, Kelsen presents parties and parliament as the necessary instruments for the formation of the will of the state. For Schmitt, such a conception is contradictory, since he believes that in democracy such a will has to be pregiven at the outset and cannot be the product of discussion. The people must be able to express its political unity directly and without mediation. It is on these grounds that he criticizes the idea of the 'social contract' since, he says, either unanimity is pregiven or it is not pregiven; where it does not exist, a contract will not bring it into being and where it does exist, there is no point in a contract.[27] Have we then no alternative but a choice between democracy as substance, with all the dangers that implies, and democracy as procedure, with the impoverishment of the concept thereby entailed? I do not believe so; in my view there are correct and useful elements in the writings of both Kelsen and Schmitt, but they need to be reinterpreted.

Kelsen is right to insist on the need for procedures which enable agreement to be achieved in conditions where a single and homogenous general will is not possible. He is, however, wrong to reduce democracy to a mere question of procedure. On the other hand, in a certain sense, Schmitt is right when he asserts that, without homogeneity, there can be no democracy. Everything depends on the way this homogeneity is conceived. In his *Verfassungslehre*, he relates it to the notion of equality and declares that the political form specific to democracy must be linked to a substantial concept of equality. This equality must be conceived as political equality; it cannot be based on a lack of distinction between persons, but must be grounded in the fact of belonging to a determinate political community. That community can, however, be defined by different criteria: race, religion, physical or moral qualities, destiny or tradition. Since the nineteenth century, says Schmitt, it has been membership of a determinate nation that has constituted the substance of democratic equality.[28] For Schmitt, the basic problem is one of political unity; for, without such unity, there can be no state. This unity must be provided by a common substance, in which the citizens share, which will enable them to be treated as equals in a democracy. What renders his conception questionable and potentially totalitarian is that he presents this homogeneity as being substantial in nature, leaving no place for pluralism. Yet it seems to me that, while accepting this need for homogeneity, one could interpret such homogeneity as being constituted by agreement on a certain number of political principles. It is identification with these principles that would provide the common substance required for democratic citizenship.

One finds a similar view in Hermann Heller who, in his critique of Schmitt's *The Concept of the Political*, acknowledges that a certain degree of social homogeneity and shared political values is necessary if democratic unity is to be achieved, but argues that this does not imply the elimination of social antagonisms. So far as parliamentarism is concerned, his reply to Schmitt is that the intellectual bases for this are to be found 'not in the belief in public discussion as such, but in the belief that a common basis for discussion exists and in the idea of fairness to the opponent, with whom one wishes to arrive at an agreement in conditions which exclude the use of brute force'.[29]

What I am proposing is that adherence to the political principles of the liberal democratic regime should be considered as the basis of homogeneity required for democratic equality. The principles in question are those of liberty and equality and it is clear that they can give rise to multiple interpretations and that no-one can pretend to possess the 'correct' interpretation. It is, therefore, essential to establish a certain number of mechanisms and procedures for arriving at decisions and for determining the will of the state within the framework of a debate on the interpretation of these principles. I am thus in partial agreement with both Schmitt and Kelsen: with the former because procedures are not deemed sufficient for creating the political unity of a democracy and a more substantial homogeneity is required; with the latter because of the view that the general will can never be immediately pregiven without the mediation of a certain number of procedures.

Such a solution would, of course, be unacceptable to Schmitt who believes in the existence of absolute truth; nor would it satisfy Kelsen since it runs counter to his 'pure theory' of law. It implies that, in the field of politics and law, one is always in the domain of power relations and that no consensus could be established as the outcome of a process of pure reasoning. Where there is power, force and violence cannot be completely eliminated, even though these may only take the form of 'force of argument' or 'symbolic violence'.

To defend political liberalism and pluralism within a perspective which is not rationalist, we have to see parliament not as the place where one accedes to truth, but as the place where it ought to be possible to reach agreement on a reasonable solution through argument and persuasion, while being aware that such agreement can never be definitive and that it should always be open to challenge. Hence the importance of re-creating, in politics, the connection with the great tradition of rhetoric, as suggested by Chaim Perelman.[30]

To accord parliament and parties a crucial role in modern democracy, in a manner that runs counter to Schmitt's critique, in no sense amounts to defending these institutions as they currently function. It is beyond doubt that they leave a great deal to be desired and that many of the defects exposed by Schmitt have since become more acute. A healthy democratic system requires a whole range of conditions, both political and economic, that are increasingly difficult to find in our societies, dominated as they are by large corporate bodies. What has to be challenged, however, is not pluralist democracy as such, as Schmitt would have it, but its limitations. And it ought to be possible to find a remedy for these.

The Limits of Pluralism

The central thesis of this article is that the whole question of modern democracy revolves around pluralism. Up to this point, Schmitt has served us as an 'indicator', showing both the force of attraction that unity-based thinking exerts and the dangers inherent in it. He may, however, also serve to put us on our guard against the excesses of a certain type of pluralism. In his discussion of Anglo-Saxon pluralist theories, he does in fact provide a series of arguments of great importance. According to pluralists like Harold Laski or G. D. H. Cole, each individual is a member of many communities and associations, none of which may have priority over the others. They thus conceive the state as an association of the same type as religious societies or professional groupings, and see individuals as having no overriding obligations to it. For Schmitt, this is a conception typical of liberal individualism, which always attributes the key role in the resolution of conflict to the individual. For his part, he takes the view that 'Only as long as the essence of the political is not comprehended or not taken into consideration is it possible to place a political association pluralistically on the same level with religious, cultural, economic, or other associations and permit it to compete with these.'[31]

Schmitt is right to insist on the specificity of the political association, and I believe we must not be led by the defence of pluralism to argue that our participation in the state as a political community is on the same level as our other forms of social integration. Any thinking on the political involves recognizing the limits of pluralism. Antagonistic principles of legitimacy cannot coexist within the same political association; there cannot be pluralism at that level without the political reality of the state automatically disappearing. But in a liberal democratic regime, this does not exclude there being cultural, religious and moral pluralism at another level, as well as a plurality of different parties. However, this pluralism requires allegiance to the state as an 'ethical state' which crystallizes the institutions and principles proper to the mode of collective existence that is modern democracy. Here we may again take up Schmitt's idea of an 'ethics laid down by the State as autonomous ethical subject, an ethics emanating from it',[32] on condition that we formulate it in terms of that new regime characterized by the articulation of democracy and liberalism.

Those who conceive the pluralism of modern democracy as a total pluralism, with the only restriction being an agreement on procedures, forget that such 'regulative' rules only have meaning in relation to 'constitutive' rules which are necessarily of another order. Far from being bound up with a 'relativist' vision of the world, as some writers have it, modern democracy requires the affirmation of a certain number of 'values' which, like equality and freedom, constitute its 'political principles'. It establishes a form of human coexistence which requires a distinction between the public and the private, the separation of Church and State, and of civil and religious law. These are some of the basic achievements of the democratic revolution and they are what make the existence of pluralism possible. One cannot therefore call these distinctions into question in the name of pluralism. Hence the problem posed by the integration of a religion like Islam, which does not accept these distinctions. Recent events surrounding the Rushdie affair show that there is a problem here which will not be easily solved. We find ourselves faced now with a real challenge: how are we to defend the greatest possible degree of pluralism while not yielding over what constitutes the essence of modern democracy? How are we to make the distinction between those values and customs in our 'public morality' that are specific to Christianity and which we therefore cannot justly impose on everyone in what has become objectively a multi-ethnic and multi-cultural society, and those values and customs that are an expression of principles without which pluralist democracy could not continue to exist? This is far from easy and doubtless there is no clear and simple answer to such a question, but it is one which must be taken into consideration in our thinking.

To understand the specificity of the liberal democratic regime as a form of society is also to grasp its historical character. Far from being an irreversible event, the democratic revolution may come under threat and has to be defended. The rise of various forms of religious fundamentalism of Christian origin in the USA and the resurgence of Catholic integrism in France indicate that the danger does not come solely from outside but also from our own tradition. The relegation of religion to the private sphere, which we now have to make Muslims accept, was only imposed with great difficulty upon the Christian Church and is still not completely accomplished. And, from a different angle, individual freedom is in a distinctly precarious position when wealth and power are concentrated in the hands of groups that are increasingly outside the control of the democratic process.

Isn't the creation of a true democratic pluralism a project which could infuse a little enthusiasm into our societies where scepticism and apathy shade into despair and revolt? To achieve this, however, a difficult balance has to be struck between, on the one hand, democracy understood as a set of procedures required to cope with plurality, and, on the other, democracy as the adherence to values which inform a particular mode of coexistence. Any attempt to give one aspect precedence over the other runs the risk of depriving us of the most precious element of this new form of government.

It is true that there is something paradoxical about modern democracy and Schmitt helps us to see this, though he also fails to understand its real significance. For him, pluralist democracy is a contradictory combination of irreconcilable principles, whereas democracy is a logic of identity and equivalence, its complete realization rendered impossible by the logic of pluralism, which constitutes an obstacle to a total system of identification. It cannot be denied that, through the articulation of liberalism and democracy, the democratic logic of equivalence has been linked with the liberal logic of difference, which tends to construe every identity as positivity, thus establishing a pluralism which subverts every attempt at totalization. These two logics are, therefore, ultimately incompatible, but this in no way means that liberal democracy is a non-viable form of government, as Schmitt declares. I believe, on the contrary, that it is the existence of this tension between the logic of identity and the logic of difference that defines the essence of pluralist democracy and makes it a form of government particularly well-suited to the undecidable character of modern politics. Far from bewailing this tension, we should be thankful for it and see it as something to be defended, not eliminated. It is this tension, in fact, which also shows up as a tension between our identities as individuals and as citizens or between the principles of freedom and equality, which constitutes the best guarantee that the project of modern democracy is alive and inhabited by pluralism. The desire to resolve it could lead only to the elimination of the political and the destruction of democracy.

Translated by Chris Turner

Notes

1. Norberto Bobbio, *La Stampa*, 9 June 1989.

2. Carl Schmitt, *The Crisis of Parliamentary Democracy*, trans. E. Kennedy, Cambridge, Mass. and London 1985, p. 34.

3. Ibid, p. 35.

4. Ibid, pp. 34–35.

5. Ibid, p. 6.

6. Ibid, p. 17.

7. Ibid, p. 35.

8. Ibid, p. 16.

9. Carl Schmitt, *Political Theology*, trans. George Schwab, Cambridge, Mass. and London 1985, p. 36.

10. On this point, see 'American Liberalism and its Communitarian Critics' in this volume.

11. Claude Lefort, *Democracy and Political Theory*, trans. D. Macey, Cambridge 1988, p. 19.

12. Carl Schmitt, *The Concept of the Political*, trans. George Schwab, New Brunswick 1976, pp. 70–71.

13. Ibid, p. 35.

14. Ibid, p. 37.

15. Hans Blumenberg, *The Legitimacy of the Modern Age*, Cambridge, Mass. 1983.

16. Ibid, p. 65.

17. Charles E. Larmore, *Patterns of Moral Complexity*, Cambridge 1987, p. 53.

18. Ronald Dworkin, 'Liberalism', in Stuart Hampshire, ed., *Public and Private Morality*, Cambridge 1978, p. 127.

19. Ibid, p. 142.

20. Ronald Dworkin, *Taking Rights Seriously*, Cambridge, Mass. 1977, p. 176.

21. Ibid, p. 182.

22. I examine this development in Rawls's work in my article 'Rawls: Political Philosophy without Politics', in this volume.

23. Ronald Dworkin, *New York Review of Books*, 17 April 1983.

24. Joseph Raz, *The Morality of Freedom*, Oxford 1986, p. 420.

25. Schmitt, *The Concept of the Political*, p. 35.

26. Kelsen's work is very extensive and highly specialized. On the subject that concerns us here, see *What is justice? Justice, Law and Politics in the Mirror of Science*, Berkeley 1957.

27. Schmitt, *The Crisis of Parliamentary Democracy*, p. 14.

28. Schmitt, *Verfassungslehre*, Munich/Leipzig 1928. This work has not been translated into English.

29. Hermann Heller, 'Politische Demokratie und soziale Homogenität', *Gesammelte Schriften*, vol. 2, Leyden 1971, p. 427. This is referred to by Ellen Kennedy in her introduction to Schmitt, *The Crisis of Parliamentary Democracy*, p. xlix.

30. For Chaim Perelman's work, see particularly *Le Champ de l'Argumentation*, Brussels 1970; *Justice et Raison*, Brussels 1972; *L'Empire rhétorique*, Paris 1977.

31. Schmitt, *The Concept of the Political*, p. 45.

32. Schmitt, 'Ethique de l'Etat et l'état pluraliste', in *Parlementarisme et démocratie*, Paris 1988, p. 148.

9

Politics and the Limits of Liberalism

The much heralded 'triumph' of liberal democracy comes at a time when there are increasing disagreements concerning its nature. Some of these disagreements concern a central tenet of liberalism: the neutrality of the state. How is this to be understood? Is a liberal society one where the state is neutral and allows the coexistence of different ways of life and conceptions of the good? Or is it a society where the state promotes specific ideals like equality or personal autonomy? Several liberals, in an attempt to respond to the communitarian challenge, have recently argued that, far from neglecting ideas about the good, liberalism is the embodiment of a set of specific values.[1]

William Galston, for instance, maintains that the three most important advocates of the neutral state, Rawls, Dworkin and Ackerman, cannot avoid reference to a substantive theory of the good, which he calls 'rationalist humanism'. He claims that, without acknowledging it, they 'covertly rely on the same triadic theory of the good, which assumes the worth of human existence, the worth of human purposiveness and of fulfilment of human purposes, and the worth of rationality as the chief constraint on social principles and actions'.[2] According to Galston, liberals should adopt a 'perfectionist' stance and state openly that liberalism promotes a specific conception of the good and is committed to the pursuit of the ends and virtues that are constitutive of the liberal polity.

While rejecting the solution of perfectionism, many liberals acknowledge the shortcomings of the neutrality thesis as it is usually formulated. This is the case with John Rawls who, in his work subsequent to *A Theory of Justice*, has clearly distanced himself from the 'priority of the right over the good' type of interpretation which his communitarian critics imputed to him. He now insists that 'Justice as fairness is not procedurally neutral. Clearly its principles of justice are substantive and express far more than procedural values, and so do its political conception of person and society, which are represented in the original position.'[3]

Ronald Dworkin, for his part, never accepted the idea of an absolute neutrality. In his view, at the very heart of liberalism lies a certain conception of equality. It is because it must treat all its members as equal that the liberal state must be neutral. Thus he asserts that, 'Since the citizens of a society differ in their conceptions [of the good life], the government does not treat them as equals if it prefers one conception to another, either because the officials believe that one is intrinsically superior, or because one is held by the more numerous or more powerful groups.'[4] For him, liberalism is based on a constitutive morality and not on scepticism. A liberal state must, he says, treat human beings as equals 'not because there is no right or wrong in political morality, but because that is what is right'.[5]

Of the three authors singled out by Galston, Bruce Ackerman is the only true 'neutralist', for he believes that what is constitutive of liberalism is a commitment to neutral dialogue and that the commitment to equality should be constrained by the conditions imposed by such a dialogue. Moreover, his conception of neutral dialogue leaves no space for philosophical inquiry into conceptions of the good and he defends the idea that liberalism should be based on scepticism since, according to him, 'there are no moral meanings hidden in the bowels of the universe.'[6]

Political Liberalism

I submit that what is really at stake in the debate about neutrality is the nature of pluralism and its place in liberal democracy. The way the liberal state is envisaged has far-reaching consequences for democratic politics. Indeed, it determines how to tackle crucial issues like that of 'multiculturalism'. My intention here is to examine what is currently the most influential position: namely, 'political liberalism', which aims at maintaining the idea of neutrality while reformulating it.

Political liberals like John Rawls and Charles Larmore[7] start from what they characterize as the 'fact' of pluralism, that is, the multiplicity of conceptions of the good that exist in modern democratic society. This leads to the 'liberal problem' of how to organize coexistence among people with different conceptions of the good. It is worth noting that they do not advocate pluralism because they believe diversity is particularly valuable, but rather because they consider it could not be eradicated without the use of state coercion. Theirs is a

Lockean kind of thinking, based more on the reasons why pluralism should not be interfered with, than on recognition of its value. Take Rawls, for instance. He defines the modern predicament as constituted by '(i) the fact of pluralism and (ii) the fact of its permanence, as well as (iii) the fact that this pluralism can be overcome only by the oppressive use of state power (which presupposes a control of the state no group possesses).'[8] Neutrality, then, is defined as non-interference with substantive views, and pluralism is identified with the toleration of different ways of life irrespective of their intrinsic value.

The critics of neutrality, on the other hand, assert that pluralism should be envisaged as an axiological principle, expressing the recognition that there are many different and incompatible ways of life that are nevertheless valuable. This is the meaning of the 'value pluralism' defended by Joseph Raz, who establishes a connection between pluralism and the ideal of personal autonomy. According to Raz, autonomy presupposes moral pluralism because it is only if a person has a variety of morally acceptable options to choose from that she can live an autonomous life. He states: 'To put it more precisely, if autonomy is an ideal then we are committed to such a view of morality: valuing autonomy leads to the endorsement of moral pluralism.'[9] Contrary to Rawls, who believes that pluralism requires the rejection of perfectionism, Raz sees a necessary link between the kind of perfectionism to which he is committed and the existence of pluralism. This allows him to conceive pluralism not merely as a 'fact' that we have grudgingly to accept, but as something to be celebrated and valued because it is the condition for personal autonomy. We can see why, from such a perspective, one more akin to John Stuart Mill than to Locke, the fostering of pluralism cannot be theorized in terms of neutrality.

'Political liberalism' claims to provide a better framework than perfectionism for accommodating the plurality of interests and visions of the good that exist in modern democratic societies. In the view of its champions, conceptions of liberalism that make reference to the good life are inadequate for that task because 'They have themselves become simply another part of the problem.'[10] How convincing is their case? Do they really offer the best perspective for envisaging the nature of a liberal democratic consensus? As I have indicated, the central concern of such conceptions is the possibility of social unity under modern conditions in which there is a multiplicity of conflicting conceptions of the good life. Rawls formulates this question in the following way: 'How is it possible that there may exist over time a stable and just society of free and equal citizens profoundly divided by reasonable though incompatible religious, philosophical and moral doctrines?'[11] It is as a solution to that problem that both Rawls and Larmore defend a liberalism that is strictly 'political' in the sense that it does not rely on any comprehensive moral ideal, on any philosophy of man of the type put forward by liberal philosophers like Kant or Mill. Their argument is that, if they are to be accepted by people who disagree about the nature of the good life, liberal institutions cannot be justified on grounds which are bound to be controversial, like ideals of Kantian autonomy or Millian individuality.

Political liberals concede to the perfectionists that the liberal state must necessarily make reference to some idea of the common good and that it cannot be neutral with respect to morality. Nevertheless – while granting that they cannot do without a theory of the good – they claim that theirs is a *minimal* theory. It should be distinguished from comprehensive views since it is a common morality which is restricted to principles that can be accepted by people who have different and conflicting ideals of the good life. According to Larmore, the proper meaning of the notion of 'neutrality' is as follows: 'Neutral principles are ones that we can justify without appealing to the controversial views of the good life to which we happen to be committed.'[12] And Rawls states that his theory of justice is a 'political' not a 'metaphysical' one, whose aim is 'to articulate a public basis of justification for the basic structure of a constitutional regime working from fundamental intuitive ideas implicit in the public political culture and abstracting from comprehensive religious, philosophical and moral doctrines. It seeks common ground – or, if one prefers, neutral ground – given the fact of pluralism.'[13]

Liberalism can, of course, offer other solutions to the problem of social unity. Some liberals consider that a Hobbesian *modus vivendi* should be enough to provide the type of consensus required by a pluralistic society. Others believe that a constitutional consensus on established legal procedures fulfils that role as effectively as would a consensus on justice. But 'political liberalism' finds those solutions wanting and proclaims the need for a *moral* type of consensus in which values and ideals play an authoritative role.

Explaining the objective of the political liberals, Larmore declares that they want to avoid appealing to controversial views of the good life, but also to scepticism, which is itself a matter of reasonable disagreement. Moreover, they are not satisfied with a type of justification based merely on strategic considerations, a Hobbesian one grounded on purely prudential motives. In Larmore's view, 'Only by finding a mean between these two extremes can liberalism work as a minimal moral conception.'[14]

In fact the ambition of 'political liberalism' is to formulate a definitive list of rights, principles and institutional arrangements that are unassailable and will create the basis of a consensus that is both moral and neutral. To that effect, these liberal thinkers propose to leave aside 'disputed' religious, philosophical and metaphysical issues and limit themselves to a strictly 'political' understanding of liberalism. This, they believe, could constitute the common ground that can still be obtained when there is no more possibility of a common good. One of their main tenets is that in a liberal society, people should not be made to accept institutions and arrangements on grounds that they could reasonably reject. Political discussion needs therefore to be constrained by rules that determine the type of convictions that can be appealed to in argumentation. Their enterprise consists in defining such a framework and hoping that it will create the conditions necessary to deliver indisputable results.

In the case of Larmore, the solution is a form of justification that relies on the two norms of rational dialogue and equal respect. For him, legitimate political principles are those which are arrived at through a rational dialogue in which the parties are moved by the norm of equal respect. This demands that we stand aside from disputed views of the good life and that we respect political neutrality when we devise principles for the political order. It implies that 'when disagreement arises, those wishing to continue the conversation should withdraw to neutral ground, in order either to resolve the dispute or, if that cannot be done rationally, to bypass it.'[15] Rawls, for his part, sees the solution in the creation of an overlapping consensus on a political conception of justice. By practising a method of 'avoidance' and ignoring philosophical and moral controversies, he hopes that a free agreement can be reached through public reason on principles of justice that 'specify a point of view from which all citizens can examine before one another whether or not their political institutions are just.'[16]

Liberalism and the Negation of the Political

The success of political liberalism hinges on the possibility of establishing the conditions for a type of argumentation that reconciles morality with neutrality. I will argue in a moment that its attempt to find a principle of social unity in a form of neutrality grounded on rationality cannot succeed. But first I want to show how the very formulation of such a project depends on evacuating the dimension of the political and conceiving the well-ordered society as one exempt from politics.

When we look at the argument closely, we see that it consists in relegating pluralism and dissent to the private sphere in order to secure consensus in the public realm. All controversial issues are taken off the agenda in order to create the conditions for a 'rational' consensus. As a result, the realm of politics becomes merely the terrain where individuals, stripped of their 'disruptive' passions and beliefs and understood as rational agents in search of self-advantage – within the constraints of morality, of course – submit to procedures for adjudicating between their claims that they consider 'fair'. This is a conception of politics in which one readily recognizes a typical case of the liberal negation of the political, such as Carl Schmitt has criticized, for whom 'liberal concepts typically move between ethics (intellectuality) and economics (trade). From that polarity they attempt to annihilate the political as a domain of conquering power and repression.'[17]

To envisage politics as a rational process of negotiation among individuals is to obliterate the whole dimension of power and antagonism – what I call 'the political' – and thereby completely miss its nature. It is also to neglect the predominant role of passions as moving forces of human conduct. Furthermore, in the field of politics, it is groups and collective identities that we encounter, not isolated individuals, and its dynamics cannot be apprehended by reducing it to individual calculations. This has devastating consequences for the liberal approach since, as Freud has taught us, while self-advantage may in certain circumstances be an important motivation for the isolated individual, it very seldom determines the conduct of groups. It is not necessary to endorse entirely Schmitt's conception of the political in order to concede the strength of his point when he exposes the shortcomings of a view that presents politics as a neutral domain insulated from all the divisive issues that exist in the private realm. The liberal claim that a universal rational consensus could be produced by an undistorted dialogue, and that free public reason could guarantee the impartiality of the state, is only possible at the cost of denying the irreducible antagonistic element present in social relations, and this can have disastrous consequences for the defence of democratic institutions. To negate the political does not make it disappear, it only leads to bewilderment in the face of its manifestations and to impotence in dealing with them.

Liberalism, in so far as it is formulated within a rationalistic and individualistic framework, is bound to be blind to the existence of the political and to delude itself with regard to the nature of politics. Indeed, it eliminates from the outset the 'differentia specifica' of politics, its handling of collective action and attempt to establish unity in a field crisscrossed with antagonisms. Liberalism overlooks the fact that it concerns the construction of collective identities and the creation of a 'we' as opposed to a 'them'. Politics, as the attempt to domesticate the political, to keep at bay the forces of destruction and to establish order, always has to do with conflicts and antagonisms. It requires an understanding that every consensus is, by necessity, based on acts of exclusion and that there can never be a fully inclusive 'rational' consensus.

This is a crucial point which the notion of the 'constitutive outside', borrowed from Derrida, can help us to elucidate. One of Derrida's central ideas is that the constitution of an identity is always based on excluding something and establishing a violent hierarchy between the resultant two poles – form/matter, essence/accident, black/white, man/woman, and so on. This reveals that there is no identity that is self-present to itself and not constructed as difference, and that any social objectivity is constituted through acts of power. It means that any social objectivity is ultimately political and has to show traces of the exclusion which governs its constitution, what we can call its 'constitutive outside'. As a consequence, all systems of social relations imply to a certain extent relations of power, since the construction of a social identity is an act of power.

Power, as Ernesto Laclau indicates, should not be conceived as an external relation taking place between two preconstituted identities, because it is power that constitutes the identities themselves. According to him, 'Systems of social organization can be seen as attempts to reduce the margin of undecidability, to make way for actions and decisions that are as coherent as possible. But by the simple fact of the presence of negativity and given the primary and constitutive character of any antagonism, the hiding of the "ultimate" undecidability of any decision will never be complete and social coherence will only be achieved at the cost of repressing something that negates it. It is in this sense that any consensus, that any objective and differential system of rules implies, as its most essential possibility, a dimension of coercion.'[18]

Rationality and Neutrality

Now, it is precisely this dimension of undecidability and coercion that 'political liberalism' is at pains to eliminate. It offers us a picture of the well-ordered society as one from which antagonism, violence, power and repression have disappeared. But, in fact, this is only because they have been made invisible through a clever stratagem.

Political liberals are, of course, perfectly aware that the pluralism they defend cannot be total and that some views will have to be excluded. Nevertheless, they justify those exclusions by declaring that they are the product of the 'free exercise of practical reason' that establishes the limits of possible consensus. It is, according to them, necessary to distinguish between 'simple' and 'reasonable pluralism'.[19] When a point of view is excluded it is because this is required by the exercise of reason. Once exclusions are presented as arising from a free agreement resulting from rational procedures ('veil of ignorance' or rational dialogue), they appear as immune from relations of power. In that way rationality is the key to solving the 'paradox of liberalism': how to eliminate its adversaries while remaining neutral.

This strategy can be seen in Larmore's project to formulate a 'neutral justification of the neutrality of the state'. He starts by identifying neutrality with a minimal moral conception: a common ground that is neutral with respect to controversial views of the good life. Next, in order to specify that common ground in a neutral way, he resorts to shared norms of equal respect and rational dialogue. According to Larmore, because the norms of equal respect and rational dialogue have been central to Western culture, it should be possible to convince the romantic critics of modern individualism that they can support a liberal political order without having to renounce their cherished values of tradition and belonging. While acknowledging the debt that his conception of 'ideal conditions of rational argument' owes to Habermas's idea of an 'ideal speech situation', he claims that his approach is more contextualist than Habermas's because his ideal conditions of justification never depart entirely from our historical circumstances and are a function of our general view of the world.[20] What Larmore has in mind, like Rawls, is the creation of an 'overlapping consensus' based on norms widely accepted in modern Western societies.

Larmore believes that, thanks to his device, he has reached principles that should be accepted by rational people interested in designing principles of political association, and that he has provided a justification for the neutrality of the state that does not depend on any controversial doctrine. But, as Galston has pointed out, besides the irony of attempting to resolve the dispute between the heirs of Kant and Mill and the neo-romantics by appealing to the Kantian conception of equal respect, Larmore's solution leaves out the increasing number of religious believers whose opposition to liberalism constitutes a much more real challenge than do the romantic critics of individualism.[21]

Larmore would probably reply that disagreements of such a kind cannot be accepted as 'reasonable'. But who decides what is and what is not 'reasonable'? In politics the very distinction between 'reasonable' and 'unreasonable' is already the drawing of a frontier; it has a political character and is always the expression of a given hegemony. What is at a given moment deemed 'rational' or 'reasonable' in a community is what corresponds to the dominant language games and the 'common sense' that they construe. It is the result of a process of 'sedimentation' of an ensemble of discourses and practices whose political character has been elided. If it is perfectly legitimate to make a distinction between the reasonable and the unreasonable, such an opposition has implications that must be acknowledged. Otherwise a specific configuration of practices and arrangements becomes naturalized and is put out of reach of critical inquiry. In a modern democracy, we should be able to question the very frontiers of reason and to put under scrutiny the claims to universality made in the name of rationality. As Judith Butler reminds us, 'To establish a set of norms that are beyond power or force is itself a powerful and forceful conceptual practice that sublimates, disguises and extends its own power play through recourse to tropes of normative universality.'[22]

The same effort to eliminate undecidability and power can be found in Rawls. Justice as fairness is presented as an acceptable basis for consensus in a pluralistic society because it is non-partisan and transcends the different comprehensive views. To be sure, Rawls now acknowledges that his theory is not transhistorical but is the answer to a specific question: namely, 'Which conception of justice is most appropriate for realizing the value of liberty and equality in basic institutions?' This of course implies that the discussion is going to be constrained by the premiss that the values of liberty and equality are the ones to be taken into account. For him, this requirement simply indicates that we start from the fundamental intuitive ideas present in our societies. He sees it as self-evident and uncontroversial, but it is not. Far from being a benign statement of fact, it is the result of a *decision* which already excludes from the dialogue those who believe that different values should be the organizing ones of the political order. Rawls, who considers that in our societies those values provide the criteria of moral reasonableness, rules out their objections. He is convinced that starting from those basic, reasonable premises, a process of neutral, rational reasoning leads to the formulation of a theory of justice that all reasonable and rational people should accept. In consequence, those who disagree with them are disqualified on the ground of being either unreasonable or irrational. This represents no problem for him since he believes that 'political institutions satisfying the principles of a liberal conception of justice realize political values and ideas that normally outweigh whatever values oppose them.'[23]

Thanks to that 'wager', he whisks away not only the role of force in upholding the rules and institutions that produce the 'overlapping consensus' but also its 'outside'.

Pluralism and Undecidability

As we can see, in order to create the conditions for successful argumentation, political liberals refuse to open rational dialogue to those who do not accept their 'rules of the game'. In a sense there is nothing objectionable about that, provided one is aware of the implications – but of course in this case the implications would defeat the very purpose of supposedly rational argumentation.

It is now generally acknowledged that argumentation is only possible when there is a shared framework. As Wittgenstein pointed out, to have agreement in opinions, there must first be agreement on the language used. But he also alerted us to the fact that those represented 'not agreement in opinions but in forms of life'.[24] In his view, to agree on the definition of a term is not enough and we need agreement in the way we use it. As he puts it: 'If language is to be a means of communication there must be agreement not only in definitions but also (queer as this may sound) in judgements.'[25]

As John Gray indicates, Wittgenstein's analysis of rules and rule-following undermines the kind of liberal reasoning that envisages the common framework for argumentation on the model of a 'neutral' or 'rational' dialogue. According to a Wittgensteinian perspective: 'Whatever there is of definite content in contractarian deliberation and its deliverance, derives from particular judgments we are inclined to make as practitioners of specific forms of life. The forms of life in which we find ourselves are themselves held together by a network of precontractual agreements, without which there would be no possibility of mutual understanding or therefore, of disagreement.'[26] Such an approach offers a fruitful alternative to rationalist liberalism because it can be developed in a way that highlights the historical and contingent character of the discourses that construct our identities. This is exemplified by Richard Flathman when he notes that, notwithstanding the fact that a good deal of agreement has been achieved on many features of liberal democratic politics, certainty is not to be seen as necessary in any of the philosophical senses. In his view, 'Our agreement in these judgments constitutes the language of our politics. It is a language arrived at and continuously modified through no less than a history of discourse, a history in which we have thought about, as we became able to think in, that language.'[27]

This is, I believe, a very promising direction for political philosophy. Contrary to the current brand of liberalism, a reflection on liberal democracy on those lines would not present it as the rational, universal solution to the problem of political order. Neither would it attempt to deny its ultimately ungrounded status by making it appear as the outcome of a rational choice or a dialogical process of undistorted communication. Because of the central role it gives to practices, such a perspective could help us understand how our shared language of politics is entangled with power and needs to be apprehended in terms of hegemonic relations. It might also leave room for 'undecidability' and be better suited to account for conflict and antagonism.

Many rationalists will certainly accuse such a political philosophy of opening the way to 'relativism' and 'nihilism' and thus jeopardizing democracy. But the opposite is true because, instead of putting our liberal institutions at risk, the recognition that they do not have an ultimate foundation creates a more favourable terrain for their defence. When we realize that, far from being the necessary result of a moral evolution of mankind, liberal democracy is an ensemble of contingent practices, we can understand that it is a conquest that needs to be protected as well as deepened.

A political philosophy that makes room for contingency and undecidability is clearly at odds with liberal rationalism, whose typical move is to erase its very conditions of enunciation and deny its historical space of inscription. This was already constitutive of the 'hypocrisy' of the Enlightenment, as Reinhart Koselleck has shown.[28] Many liberals follow suit by refusing to assume their political stand and pretending to be speaking from an impartial location. In that way they manage to present their views as the embodiment of 'rationality' and this enables them to exclude their opponents from 'rational dialogue'. However, the excluded do not disappear and, once their position has been declared 'unreasonable', the problem of neutrality remains unsolved. From their point of view, the 'neutral' principles of rational dialogue are certainly not so. For them, what is proclaimed as 'rationality' by the liberals is experienced as coercion.

It is not my intention to advocate a total pluralism and I do not believe it is possible to avoid excluding some points of view. No state or political order, even a liberal one, can exist without some forms of exclusion. My point is different. I want to argue that it is very important to recognize those forms of exclusion for what they are and the violence that they signify, instead of concealing them under the veil of rationality. To disguise the real nature of the necessary 'frontiers' and modes of exclusion required by a liberal democratic order by grounding them in the supposedly neutral character of 'rationality' creates effects of occultation which hinder the proper workings of democratic politics. William Connolly is right when he indicates that 'the pretense to neutrality functions to maintain established settlements below the threshold of public discourse.'[29]

The specificity of pluralist democracy does not reside in the absence of domination and violence but in the establishment of a set of institutions through which they can be limited and contested. It is for that reason that democracy 'maintains a split between law and justice: it accepts the fact that justice is "impossible", that it is an act which can never be wholly grounded in "sufficient (legal) reasons".'[30] But this mechanism of 'self-binding' ceases to be effective if violence goes unrecognized and hidden behind appeals to rationality. Hence the importance of abandoning the mystifying illusion of a dialogue free from coercion. It might undermine democracy by closing the gap between justice and law which is a constitutive space of modern democracy.

In order to avoid the danger of such a closure, what must be relinquished is the very idea that there could be such a thing as a 'rational' political consensus, if that means a consensus that would not be based on any form of exclusion. To present the institutions of liberal democracy as the outcome of a pure deliberative rationality is to reify them and make them impossible to transform. The fact that, like any other regime, modern pluralist democracy constitutes a system of relations of power, is denied and the democratic challenging of those forms of power becomes illegitimate.

The political liberalism of Rawls and Larmore, far from being conducive to a pluralistic society, manifests a strong tendency toward homogeneity and leaves little space for dissent and contestation in the sphere of politics. By postulating that it is possible to reach a free moral consensus on political fundamentals through rational procedures and that such a consensus is provided by liberal institutions, it ends up endowing a historically specific set of arrangements with the character of universality and rationality. This is contrary to the indetermination that is constitutive of modern democracy. In the end, the rationalist defence of liberalism, by searching for an argument that is beyond argumentation and by wanting to define the meaning of the universal, makes the same mistake for which it criticizes totalitarianism: it rejects democratic indeterminacy and identifies the universal with a given particular.

Modern democratic politics, linked as it is to the declaration of human rights, does indeed imply a reference to universality. But this universality is conceived as a horizon that can never be reached. Every pretension to occupy the place of the universal, to fix its final meaning through rationality, must be rejected. The content of the universal must remain indeterminate since it is this indeterminacy that is the condition of existence of democratic politics.

The specificity of modern democratic pluralism is lost when it is envisaged merely as the empirical fact of a multiplicity of moral conceptions of the good. It needs to be understood as the expression of a symbolic mutation in the ordering of social relations: the democratic revolution envisaged in Claude Lefort's terms as 'the dissolution of the markers of certainty'. In a modern democratic society there can be no longer a substantive unity and division must be recognized as constitutive. It is 'a society in which Power, Law and Knowledge are exposed to a radical indeterminacy, a society that has become the theatre of an uncontrollable adventure.'[31]

Morality, Unanimity and Impartiality

What has been celebrated as a revival of political philosophy in the last decades is in fact a mere extension of moral philosophy; it is moral reasoning applied to the treatment of political institutions. This is manifest in the absence in current liberal theorizing of a proper distinction between moral discourse and political discourse. To recover the normative aspect of politics, moral concerns about impartiality and unanimity are introduced into political argumentation. The result is a public morality for liberal societies, a morality which is deemed to be 'political' because it is 'minimal' and avoids engaging with controversial conceptions of the good and because it provides the cement for social cohesion.[32]

There might well be a place for such an endeavour, but it cannot replace political philosophy and it does not provide us with the adequate understanding of the political that we urgently need. Moreover, its insistence on universalism and individualism can be harmful because it masks the real challenge that a reflection on pluralism faces today with the explosion of nationalisms and the multiplication of particularisms. Those phenomena need to be grasped in political terms, as forms of construction of a 'we/them' opposition, and consequently appeals to universality, impartiality and individual rights miss the mark.

The problems arising from the conflation of morality and politics are evident in the work of another liberal: Thomas Nagel. According to him, the difficulty for political theory is that 'political institutions and their theoretical justification try to externalize the demands of the impersonal standpoint. But they have to be staffed and supported and brought to life by individuals for whom the impersonal standpoint coexists with the personal, and this has to be reflected in their design.'[33] Nagel believes that in order to be able to defend the acceptability of a political order, we need to reconcile an impartial concern for everyone with a view of how each individual can reasonably be expected to live. Nagel proposes that we should start with the conflict that each individual encounters in himself between the impersonal standpoint that produces a powerful demand for universal impartiality and equality and the personal standpoint that gives rise to individualistic motives which impede the realization of those ideals.

Central to political theory, in his view, is the question of political legitimacy, which requires the achievement of unanimity over the basic institutions of society. Like Rawls and Larmore, he rejects a Hobbesian solution because it does not integrate the impersonal standpoint and only considers personal motives and values, and he insists that some form of impartiality must be central to the pursuit of legitimacy. However, he considers that a legitimate system will have to reconcile the principle of impartiality with one of reasonable partiality so that no one could object that the demands made on them are excessive.

With their insistence on 'partiality', Nagel's views represent, no doubt, progress with respect to the position of those liberals who equate the moral point of view with that of impartiality, and privilege it at the expense of all kinds of personal commitments. The problem is the emphasis he puts on unanimity and on his search for principles that no one could reasonably reject and that all could agree that everyone should follow. He sees the strength of such principles in the fact that they will have a moral character. As a consequence, he argues that when a system is legitimate, 'those living under it have no grounds for complaint against the way its basic structure accommodates their point of view, and no one is morally justified in withholding his cooperation from the functioning of the system, trying to subvert its results, or trying to overturn it if he has the power to do so.'[34]

We find again, stated openly in this case, the same attempt to foreclose the possibility of dissent in the public realm that we have already observed in Rawls and Larmore. For those liberals, a fully realized liberal democratic order is one in which there is perfect unanimity concerning political arrangements and total coincidence between the individuals and their institutions. Their aim is to reach a type of consensus which, by its very nature, will disqualify every move to destabilize it. The pluralism they defend only resides in the private sphere and is restricted to philosophical, moral and religious issues. They do not seem to understand that there can also be unresolvable conflicts in the field of political values.

It must be said that Nagel is not very sanguine about the possibility of realizing the type of consensus he promotes, but he entertains no doubt about its desirability. He declares: 'It would be morally preferable, and a condition of true political legitimacy, if the general principles governing agent-relative reasons limited the reach of those reasons in such a way that they left standing some solutions or distributions of advantages and disadvantages that no one could reasonably refuse, even if he were in a position to do so. Instead of morality being like politics in its sensitivity to the balance of power, we should want politics to be more like morality in its aim of unanimous acceptability.'[35] This is, in my view, a dangerously misguided perspective, and people committed to democracy should be wary of all projects that aspire to create unanimity. Speaking about moral philosophy, Stuart Hampshire warns us that, 'Whether it is Aristotelian, Kantian, Humean, or utilitarian, moral philosophy can do harm when it implies that there ought to be, and that there can be, fundamental agreement on, or even a convergence in, moral ideals – the harm is that the reality of conflict, both within individuals and within societies, is disguised by the myth of humanity as a consistent moral unit across time and space. There is a false blandness in the myth, an aversion from reality.'[36] I think the same reasoning applies even more to political philosophy and that a democratic pluralist position cannot aim at establishing once and for all the definite principles and arrangements that the members of a well-ordered society should accept. Divisive issues cannot be confined to the sphere of the private, and it is an illusion to believe that it is possible to create a nonexclusive public sphere of rational argument where a noncoercive consensus could be attained. Instead of trying to erase the traces of power and exclusion, democratic politics requires that they be brought to the fore, making them visible so that they can enter the terrain of contestation.

Tackled from such a perspective, the question of pluralism is much more complex. It cannot be envisaged only in terms of already existing subjects and restricted to their conceptions of the good. What must be addressed is the very process of constitution of the subjects of pluralism. This is indeed where the more crucial issues lie today. And this is where the limitations of the current liberal approach – informed by essentialism and individualism – can have really damaging political consequences for democratic politics.[37]

What Kind of Consensus?

I agree with political liberals on the need to distinguish between liberalism as a comprehensive doctrine, a philosophy of man, and liberalism as a doctrine that is concerned with the institutions and values of the liberal society. And I am also committed – although in a way that differs from them – to elucidating the political dimension of liberalism. I want to scrutinize its contribution to the emergence of modern democracy as a new regime. But this requires recognition that the liberal democratic regime is not exhausted by its liberal component. For it consists in the articulation of two elements, the liberal one constituted by the institutions of the liberal state (rule of law, separation of powers, defence of individual rights) and the democratic one of popular sovereignty and majority rule. Moreover, liberty and equality, which constitute the political principles of the liberal democratic regime, can be interpreted in many different ways and ranked according to different priorities. This accounts for the multiple possible forms of liberal democracy. The 'liberals' privilege the values of liberty and individual rights, while the 'democrats' insist on equality and participation. But as long as neither side attempts to suppress the other, we are witnessing a struggle *inside* liberal democracy, over its priorities, and not one between alternative regimes.

To state, as Larmore does, that 'Liberalism and democracy are separate values whose relation . . . consists largely in democratic self-government being the best means for protecting the principles of a liberal political order',[38] is typically a liberal interpretation and is open to challenge. To be sure, the relation between liberalism and democracy has long been a controversial issue and will probably never be settled. A pluralist democracy is constantly pulled in opposite directions: towards exacerbation of differences and disintegration on one side; towards homogenization and strong forms of unity on the other. I consider, as I have argued elsewhere,[39] that the specificity of modern democracy as a new political form of society, as a new 'regime', lays precisely in the *tension* between the democratic logic of equality and the liberal logic of liberty. It is a tension that we should value and protect, rather than try to resolve, because it is constitutive of pluralist democracy. This does not mean that it does not create some specific problems; since the articulation between liberalism and democracy has been established, a recurrent concern of liberals has been how to put individual rights outside the reach of majoritarianism. To that effect they have wanted to put constraints on the democratic process of decision-making. Without being openly acknowledged, this is I believe one of the subtexts of the present discussion. Presenting liberal institutions as the outcome of a purely deliberative rationality might be seen as an attempt to provide them with a ground that forecloses the possibility of reasonable disagreement. This could be seen as a way to protect them against potential threats from democratic majorities.

There is, no doubt, a need to secure pluralism, individual rights and minorities against a possible majority tyranny. But the opposite danger also exists, of thereby naturalizing a given set of 'liberties' and existing rights, and at the same time buttressing many relations of inequality. The search for 'guarantees' can lead to the very destruction of pluralist democracy. Hence the importance of understanding that for democracy to exist no social agent should be able to claim any mastery of the *foundation* of society. The relation between social agents can only be termed 'democratic' in so far as they accept the particularity and the limitations of their claims – that is, only in so far as they recognize their mutual relations as ones from which power is ineradicable. This is why I have argued that the liberal evasion of the dimension of power is fraught with risks for democratic politics.

Like the exponents of 'political liberalism', I would like to see the creation of a wide consensus around the principles of pluralist democracy. But I do not believe that such a consensus should be grounded on rationality and unanimity or that it should manifest an impartial point of view. The real task, in my view, is to foster allegiance to our democratic institutions, and the best way to do this is not by demonstrating that they would be chosen by rational agents 'under the veil of ignorance' or in a 'neutral dialogue', but by creating strong forms of identification with them. This should be done by developing and multiplying in as many social relations as possible the discourses, the practices, the 'language games' that produce democratic 'subject positions'. The objective is to establish the hegemony of democratic values and practices.

This has to be envisaged as an 'ethico-political' enterprise, one that concerns the specific values that can be realized in the realm of politics through collective action, and which does not deny the constitutive role of conflict and antagonism and the fact that division is irreducible. This last point indicates why 'value pluralism' in its multiple dimensions has to be taken seriously by political philosophers. We need to make room for the pluralism of cultures, collective forms of life and regimes, as well as for the pluralism of subjects, individual choices and conceptions of the good. This has very important consequences for politics. For, in the realm of politics, once the plurality of values is granted along with their conflicting nature, undecidability cannot be the last word. Politics calls for *decision* and, despite the impossibility of finding a *final* grounding, any type of political regime consists in establishing a hierarchy among political values. A liberal democratic regime, while fostering pluralism, cannot equate all values, since its very existence as a political form of society requires a specific ordering of values which precludes a total pluralism. A political regime is always a case of 'undecidable decided' and this is why it cannot exist without a 'constitutive outside'.

Rawls indirectly points to this fact when he explains that 'a liberal view removes from the political agenda the most divisive issues.'[40] What is this, if not the drawing of a frontier between what is negotiable in a liberal society and what is not negotiable? What is this, if not a *decision* that establishes a distinction between the private and public spheres? No wonder that this process is experienced as coercion by those who do not accept such a separation. The advent of liberal pluralism as well as its continuance must be envisaged as a form of political intervention in a conflictual field, an intervention that implies the repression of other alternatives. Those other alternatives might be displaced and marginalized by the apparently irresistible march of liberal democracy, but they will never disappear completely and some of them can be reactivated. Our values, our institutions and way of life constitute one form of political order among a plurality of possible ones, and the consensus they command cannot exist without an 'outside' that will forever leave our liberal democratic values and our conception of justice open to challenge. For those who oppose these values – those who are disqualified as 'unreasonable' by our rationalist liberals and who do not participate in their overlapping consensus – the conditions imposed by the 'rational' dialogue are unacceptable because they deny some of the defining features of their identity. They might be forced to accept a *modus vivendi* but it is not one that will necessarily develop into a stable and enduring overlapping consensus as Rawls hopes. According to him, the liberal regime is a *modus vivendi* made necessary by the fact of pluralism. Yet it is a *modus vivendi* that he wants us to value and accept for moral not prudential reasons. But what about those who oppose the very idea of such a *modus vivendi*? There is obviously no place for their demands *inside* a liberal *modus vivendi*, even one whose scope would have been widened. Liberalism, for them, is a *modus vivendi* that they are forced to accept at the same time that it rejects their values.

I think there is no way to avoid such a situation and we have to face its implications. A project of radical and plural democracy has to come to terms with the dimension of conflict and antagonism within the political and has to accept the consequences of the irreducible plurality of values. This must be the starting point of our attempt to radicalize the liberal democratic regime and to extend the democratic revolution to an increasing number of social relations. Instead of shying away from the component of violence and hostility inherent in social relations, the task is to think how to create the conditions under which those aggressive forces can be defused and diverted and a pluralist democratic order made possible.

Notes

1. Some recent titles indicative of this trend are: Nancy L. Rosenblum, ed., *Liberalism and the Moral Life*, Cambridge, Mass. 1989; R. B. Douglass, G. Mara and H. Richardson, eds, *Liberalism and the Good*, New York 1990; Stephen Macedo, *Liberal Virtues. Citizenship, Virtue and Community in Liberal Constitutionalism*, Oxford 1991; William A. Galston, *Liberal Purposes. Goods, Virtues and Diversity in the Liberal State*, Cambridge 1991.

2. William A. Galston, *Liberal Purposes*, p. 92.

3. John Rawls, *Political Liberalism*, New York 1993, p. 192.

4. Ronald Dworkin, 'Liberalism', in Stuart Hampshire, ed., *Public and Private Morality*, Cambridge 1978, p. 127.

5. Ibid., p. 142.

6. Bruce Ackerman, *Social Justice and the Liberal State*, New Haven 1989, p. 368.

7. There are significant differences between Rawls and Larmore, but both defend a version of 'political liberalism' which has enough points in common to justify treating them under the same rubric.

8. John Rawls, 'The Idea of an Overlapping Consensus', *Oxford Journal of Legal Studies*, vol. 7, no. 1, p. 22.

9. Joseph Raz, *The Morality of Freedom*, Oxford 1986, p. 399.

10. Charles Larmore, 'Political Liberalism', *Political Theory*, vol. 18, no. 3, August 1990, p. 345.

11. Rawls, *Political Liberalism*, p. xviii.

12. Larmore, 'Political Liberalism', p. 341.

13. Rawls, *Political Liberalism*, p. 192.

14. Larmore, 'Political Liberalism,' p. 346.

15. Charles E. Larmore, *Patterns of Moral Complexity*, Cambridge 1987, p. 59.

16. Rawls, 'The Idea of an Overlapping Consensus', p. 5.

17. Carl Schmitt, *The Concept of the Political*, New Brunswick 1976, p. 71.

18. Ernesto Laclau, *New Reflections on the Revolution of Our Time*, London 1990, p. 172.

19. This distinction was first formulated by Joshua Cohen in 'Moral Pluralism and Political Consensus', in D. Copp and J. Hampton, *The Idea of Democracy*, Cambridge 1993. Rawls has since then made extensive use of it in his recent book *Political Liberalism*.

20. Larmore, *Patterns of Moral Complexity*, p. 56.

21. Galston, *Liberal Purposes*, p. 299.

22. Judith Butler, 'Contingent Foundations: Feminism and the Question of "Postmodernism"', in J. Butler and J. Scott, eds, *Feminists Theorize the Political*, New York and London 1992, p. 7.

23. John Rawls, 'The idea of an Overlapping Consensus', *Oxford Journal of Legal Studies*, 7, 1987, p. 24.

24. Ludwig Wittgenstein, *Philosophical Investigations*, I, 241, Oxford 1958.

25. Ibid., I, 242.

26. John Gray, *Liberalisms: Essays in Political Philosophy*, London and New York 1989, p. 252.

27. Richard E. Flathman, *Toward a Liberalism*, Ithaca and London 1989, p. 63.

28. Reinhart Koselleck, *Critique and Crisis: Enlightenment and the Pathogenesis of Modern Society*, Cambridge, Mass. 1988.

29. William E. Connolly, *Identity/Difference. Democratic Negotiations of Political Paradox*, Ithaca and London 1991, p. 161.

30. Renata Salecl, 'Democracy and Violence', *New Formations*, no. 14, Summer 1991, p. 24.

31. Claude Lefort, *The Political Forms of Modern Society*, Cambridge 1986, p. 305.

32. I have developed this aspect of my critique in 'Rawls: Political Philosophy without Politics', in this volume.

33. Thomas Nagel, *Equality and Partiality*, Oxford 1991, p. 5.

34. Ibid., p. 35.

35. Ibid., p. 45.

36. Stuart Hampshire, *Morality and Conflict*, Cambridge, Mass. 1983, p. 155.

37. On this issue, see the stimulating article by Kirstie MacClure, 'On the Subject of Rights: Pluralism, Plurality and Political Identity', in Chantal Mouffe, ed., *Dimensions of Radical Democracy*, London 1992.

38. Larmore, 'Political Liberalism', p. 359.

39. See my 'Pluralism and Modern Democracy: Around Carl Schmitt', in this volume.

40. Rawls, *Political Liberalism*, p. 157.

Index

AVAILABLE IN THE RADICAL THINKERS SERIES

AVAILABLE IN THE RADICAL THINKERS SERIES

Sexuality in the Field
of Vision

JACQUELINE ROSE

Paperback 1 84467 058 9
$12/£6/$14CAN
272 pages • 5 x 7.75 inches

The Information Bomb
PAUL VIRILIO

Paperback 1 84467 059 7
$12/£6/$14CAN
160 pages • 5 x 7.75 inches

Culture and Materialism

RAYMOND WILLIAMS

Paperback 1 84467 060 0
$12/£6/$14CAN
288 pages • 5 x 7.75 inches

The Metastases of
Enjoyment:
Six Essays on Women and
Causality
SLAVOJ ŽIŽEK

Paperback 1 84467 061 9
$12/£6/$14CAN
240 pages • 5 x 7.75 inches